Gender and Migration

Edited by Caroline Sweetman

Oxfam

The books in Oxfam's *Focus on Gender* series were originally published as single issues of the journal *Gender and Development,* which is published by Oxfam three times a year. It is the only European journal to focus specifically on gender and development issues internationally, to explore the links between gender and development initiatives, and to make the links between theoretical and practical work in this field. For information about subscription rates, please apply to Routledge Publishing, T & F Informa UK Ltd., Sheepen Place, Colchester, Essex, OC3 3LP, UK. Tel: +44 (0) 207 017 5544; Fax: +44 (0) 207 017 5198. In North America, please apply to Routledge Publishing, Taylor and Francis Inc., Customer Services Department, 325 Chestnut Street, 8th Floor, Philadelphia, PA 19106, USA; Fax +1 800 821 8312.

journal.orders@tandf.co.uk
www.tandf.co.uk/journals

Front cover: *Tamil returnees on a bus to a repatriation camp, Sri Lanka*
Photo: Howard Davies, Oxfam

First published by Oxfam GB in 1998

This edition transferred to print-on-demand in 2007

© Oxfam GB 1998

ISBN 978 0 85598 399 X

A catalogue record for this publication is available from the British Library.

Available from:
Bournemouth English Book Centre, PO Box 1496, Parkstone, Dorset, BH12 3YD, UK
tel: +44 (0)1202 712933; fax: +44 (0)1202 712930; email: oxfam@bebc.co.uk

USA: Stylus Publishing LLC, PO Box 605, Herndon, VA 20172-0605, USA
tel: +1 (0)703 661 1581; fax: +1 (0)703 661 1547; email: styluspub@aol.com

For details of local agents and representatives in other countries, consult our website:
www.oxfam.org.uk/publications
or contact Oxfam Publishing, Oxfam House, John Smith Drive, Cowley, Oxford, OX4 2JY, UK
tel +44 (0) 1865 472255; fax (0) 1865 472393; email: publish@oxfam.org.uk

Our website contains a fully searchable database of all our titles, and facilities for secure on-line ordering.

Published by Oxfam GB, Oxfam House, John Smith Drive, Cowley, Oxford, OX4 2JY, UK

Oxfam GB is a registered charity, no. 202918, and is a member of Oxfam International.

Contents

Editorial

Organisations concerned with human development are increasingly aware of the need to develop ways of working with people who are mobile, moving across local boundaries or national borders, and out of the jurisdiction of local and national governments and NGOs. How can organisations respond effectively and coherently to the needs of the growing numbers of women and men who make their living using economic and social strategies which operate in different locations? Migration's 'new global character needs to be analysed with new theoretical tools' (Hammar and Tamas 1997, 1).

The collection of articles here uses gender analysis as one such essential tool. International and national migration cannot be fully understood until 'women become visible both in terms of statistics and as major actors in the migration process' (Zlotnik 1995 252, quoted in Bjeren 1997). Looking at every facet of the livelihoods of individual women and men reveals the range of different experiences of migration. Articles here focus on labour migration, migration as a family member, and forced migration in times of conflict. Migration may take place on a temporary basis, as a part of a cycle, or as a one-off permanent movement. Several articles focus on life for migrant communities in the receiving country, examining the complex dynamics of living between and within two locations.

Focusing on human livelihoods also shows the inadequacy of, on the one hand, analyses which over-emphasise the importance of macro-economic structures, and portray people as 'forced' to migrate. The converse — analyses which see potential migrants as having a completely free choice in decisions to move — are of equally limited vaue. As Ben Rogaly's article in this issue shows, structural factors and individual agency both contribute to decisions to migrate — as he puts it, both 'compulsion' and 'choice'. Ben Rogaly's article also demonstrates that social factors as well as hard economics play an essential part in determining who migrates, and the action of migrating in turn has a social, as well as economic, outcome. Migration is determined by household or family resources and decision-making structures, the culture of the community and by the 'socially determined, gender segregated labour markets available' (Chant and Radcliffe 1992, 23).

Looking at households and social networks

While economics plays a critical role in determining people's decisions to migrate, this is not the whole story. Bringing a gender analysis to studies of migration highlights the fact that human existence depends not only on production, but on reproduction: the unremunerated work of caring for dependents, which is (in most societies) primarily the work of women. In this light, migration is part of a livelihood strategy not of an individual but of a family, developed to suit needs at a particular time. Therefore, a gender analysis also means that we focus on those individuals and families who don't migrate, as well as examining those who do. 'The individual woman's or man's migration path can only make sense in the light of what went before... and what goes on simultaneously — the divisions of duties and tasks at different locations between genders and generations' (Bjeren 1997, 245).

Recently, exciting new work on gender and migration has moved on further, to question conventional definitions of the household which focus on one physical location. In the context of absent family members contributing economically and socially, such conventional definitions of household and family are of questionable use (Bjeren 1997). Looking at the inter-relationships of the women and men involved in migration and the different kinds of work they do turns the focus onto what Nici Nelson has called the 'social field' which exists between 'the original home, the new home, the people left behind, the people encountered' (Nelson 1992, 109). It is relationships that matter: between migrants and their relatives, friends, and the wider community, in different geographical locations, and over time.

For feminists, a gender analysis of migration does not limit itself to exploring the practical conditions of women's and men's migration, but relates these to the scope offered by different experiences of migration for positive (or negative) change to women's power and status vis-à-vis the men in their community (Palmer 1985). Here, Lina Payne's article discusses these issues in the context of forced migration of displaced Sudanese women and men to Ikafe, Uganda. Her article looks at the long- as well as short-term impact of food insecurity, linking the stresses of forced migration with changes in the practical conditions of women's and men's work, and discussing how these in turn led to changes in the incidence of marital violence and family breakdown. Besides negative changes there was also a certain sense of liberation from traditional interdependence on family; as one woman put it, 'my husband is now UNHCR'.

The gendered nature of migrant work

In the absence of a gender analysis, migrants have generally been assumed either to be male and journeying in search of employment, or to be female migrating for marriage (Chant and Radcliffe 1992). Migration upon marriage is in a sense a familiar concept to women all over the world, wherever there have been norms of patrilocality (the practice of moving upon marriage to the home of your husband). In contrast, women's migration for work (and men's migration as marital partners!) has remained effectively invisible in many accounts of how and why migration occurs.

Both female and male migration for paid work is shaped by gender-based expectations of the types of work each sex should do. Women's whole rationale for migration for work, indeed, 'can be seen as an extension of their motherly and wifely responsibilities, since they went to enhance the well-being of their children, husbands and other close kin' (Bjeren 1997, 242). Most women's income-generating work is in sectors which are gendered female (Chant and Radcliffe 1992); either because the work is similar to work performed in the home — for example, domestic work or sexual services — or where the skills required can be seen as 'natural' feminine attributes (Elson and Pearson 1981).

In this issue, two articles look at the experience of women migrant domestic workers, whose work is among the least regulated in the world. Joanna Kerr and Nona Grandea examine the experience of Filipina women in Canada, exploring possible organisational responses to women's own assessment of their needs as international migrants. A parallel case is discussed by Lina Abu Habib, focusing on Sri Lankan women migrating to Lebanon. Both articles discuss the lack of response to the appalling conditions faced by migrant domestic workers. The lack of legal redress suffered by domestic workers is aggravated if they are working in a foreign country, due to their precarious status as economic migrants. These issues are explored further in Francine Pickup's article, which focuses on trafficking of women and forced prostitution in the context of Russia.

Changing places; changing perspectives

Words including 'location' and 'position' are used by social scientists to denote more than one's physical position; they can be used in a social sense to emphasise the link between one's view of life, and the experiences in different geographical and historical situations which have shaped this (Sizoo 1997).

Undoubtedly, travel and migration expose both women and men to new experiences which present opportunities for personal development(Davin 1996, in the context of China). However, colonial and post-colonial assumptions that have equated such 'development' with progress along a straight course leading to European-style 'modernity' have now been widely condemned. Rather, 'development' is now seen as a 'multidirectional process rather than something which can be defined in terms of subsequent stages or levels' (Hammar and Tamas 1997, 18).

In their article, Uma Kothari and Emma Crewe examine these issues, exploring the search for 'modernity' of Gujeratis now living in Britain, who have experienced two processes of migration — from India to Africa and from Africa to Britain. For this community, which had been prosperous in India, 'progress' through migration was understood much more widely than the opportunity to earn money. Respondents felt that on moving to Britain, overall losses as well as gains have been made.

How does 'changing places' change the women who move? Many societies place formal or informal restrictions on women's mobility. While the restrictions may be attributed to concerns for their safety, they also limit women's chances of exposure to other ways of being and doing. Women (and men) who have lived in more than one location in the world know that cultural difference is constructed by people, rather than 'natural', and can therefore question stratified gender roles

in these terms. However, no assumptions can be made that alternative ways of doing things will be seen as more desirable.

Women living in minority communities, as first- or second-generation migrants, face particular tensions in their efforts to forge a sense of identity which bridges the gap between two cultures. Women may decide to conform to cultural norms as a reaction to the pressures of living in an alien environment. Women's behaviour 'plays a pivotal role in upholding cherished cultural values' (El Solh 1993, 33). This could be seen as a positive decision; while popular images in countries with immigrant communities has tended to depict women as passive victims of culture, in fact, different women show incredible resourcefulness in adapting their behaviour in a variety of ways to new settings (ibid).

Working with migrant populations

The policy of all states and the majority of NGOs tends to target interventions to geographically limited areas, and over uninterrupted periods of time. As Ben Rogaly's article observes in the context of India, this has the consequence of marginalising seasonal wage-workers from development: 'they and their children are often excluded from geographically targeted interventions by their absence' (Rogaly, this issue).

Interventions could conceivably be targeted differently, to meet the needs of mobile populations. However, policies reflect the power relations, values, and prejudices of the surrounding society (Rao and Stuart, 1997). In her article focusing on the political, economic, and social marginalisation of partly-nomadic Roma people now located around Tuzla, Bosnia, Alex Jones analyses how widespread prejudice against Roma people among wider society has been reflected not only in inadequate provision of state services before the war, but also in the terms of the post-conflict peace agreement brokered by the international community.

Where international agreement on an issue is needed, the separate interests of different states militate against this. While new migration flows 'go mainly between countries in the South..., the flows towards the North face increasingly restrictive immigration control' (Hammar and Tamas 1997, 1). Francine Pickup's article on trafficking provides a clear example of this, discussing the varied agendas of different parts of the feminist movement, governments, and local and international NGOs, in the context of a report on a recent conference to discuss the trafficking of Russian women.

Conclusion

Integrating a gender perspective fully into development work means that agencies can no longer characterise men as migrating to an urban area for paid labour and bringing back income and progressive ideas to the rural sending area, and women as staying at home. This needs to be replaced by a more mature awareness of the many different forms that migration takes, the different people who migrate, and the effects of their migration on social and economic conditions in both sending and receiving areas.

This more complex understanding would reduce the likelihood of development interventions which make simplistic assumptions about the scope for the empowerment of women living on their own, without considering the tendency of gender ideologies to survive practical changes to women's and men's lives. In various African settings, much stress has been placed on the scope for women's empowerment offered by male absence in the mines of South Africa (Palmer 1981); however, this kind of *de facto* female-headedness leads to stress, confusion and friction in decision-making (Nelson 1992 in the context of Kenya, Sweetman 1995 in the context of Lesotho).

Far from being a one-way process of 'modernisation', different cultural influences melt into each other to form new realities as they come into contact. As far as gender relations and women's status is concerned, this new understanding simply emphasises the need to examine each case of migration individually. No one theory can encapsulate

the varied effects of migration and exposure to different cultural norms and ways of life on women and men's attitudes to gender relations and roles.

Understanding the details of different migration experiences through comprehensive research offers the only way forward to address the interests of people whose way of life is dynamic; arrivals, departures, temporary absences, and the sending of remittances are all features of migration which are not necessarily picked up by conventional methods of project design. It is essential to understand households as dynamic social networks; not all members are necessarily there at any one time, and not all present members are there throughout the year, or over a substantial period. In addition, livelihood strategies must be seen as made up of the activities of absent as well as present members of a social network.

Finally, as stated above in the context of Alex Jones' article on Romas in Bosnia, experiences of racism, directed at both sexes in minority communities, means that a shared ethnicity or nationality may be experienced more powerfully than discrimination based on grounds of gender identity (Yuval-Davis 1997). As Uma Kothari and Emma Crewe observe in their article, there is 'an eerie silence about racism' in agencies working in international development which urgently needs to be broken.

References

Bjeren G, 'Gender and reproduction' in Hammar T, Brochmann G, Tamas K and Faisi T (eds), *International Migration, Immobility and Development: Multidisciplinary Perspectives*, Berg:UK, 1997

Brydon L 'Gender and migration' in Brydon L and Chant S *Women in the Third World: gender issues in rural and urban areas*, Edward Elgar:UK 1989

Chant S and Radcliffe S, 'Migration and development: the importance of gender' in Chant S and Radcliffe S, *Gender and Migration in Developing Countries*, Belhaven Press:UK, 1992

6

Davin, D 'Gender and rural-urban migration in China', *Gender and Development* 4:1, 1996.

Elson D and Pearson R, 'The Subordination of Women and the Internationalisation of Factory Production' in Young K, Wolkowitz C and McCullagh R (eds) *Of Marriage and the Market*, CSE Books:UK, 1981

El Solh C, '"Be true to your culture": gender tensions among Somali Muslims in Britain' in *Immigrants and Minorities* 12:1, 1993

Hammar T and Tamas K, 'Why do People Go or Stay?' in Hammar T, Brochmann G, Tamas K and Faisi T (eds), *International Migration, Immobility and Development: Multidisciplinary Perspectives*, Berg:UK, 1997

Nelson N, 'Rural-Urban Migration in Central and Western Kenya' in Chant S and Radcliffe S, op. cit. 1992

Palmer I, *The Impact of Male Out-Migration on Women in Farming* Kumarian Press, 1985

Rao, A and Stuart, R 'Rethinking organisations: a feminist perspective', *Gender and Development* 5:1, 1997

Sizoo E, *Women's Lifeworlds: women's narratives on shaping their realities*, Routledge:UK, 1997

Sweetman C, *The Miners Return: Changing Gender Relations in Lesotho's Ex-Migrants' Families* University of East Anglia:UK 1995

Yuval-Davis N, *Gender and Nation*, Sage:UK, 1997

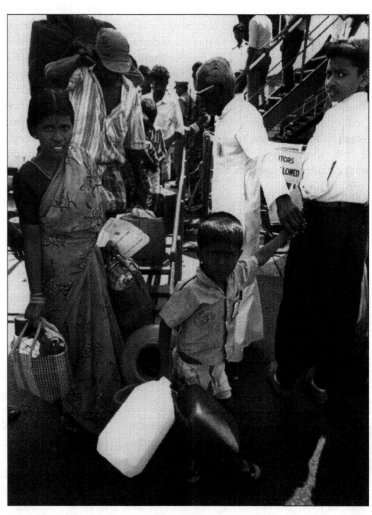

Right
Tamil returnees on their
way to a repatriation camp
in Sri Lanka

Howard Davies/Oxfam

'Frustrated and displaced':

Filipina domestic workers in Canada

Nona Grandea with Joanna Kerr

This article examines the case of Filipina domestic workers in Canada, based on a participatory action research study that the authors carried out with Filipina domestic workers in 1996. The Philippines has been a major supplier of migrant labour, and is one of the principal sources of foreign domestic workers in Canada.

In 1995, the plight of two Filipina domestic workers caught the world's attention. Flor Contemplacion was executed in Singapore for a crime many believe she did not commit. Fifteen-year old Sarah Balabagan was sentenced to death by a court in the United Arab Emirates for stabbing her male employer in self-defence. These cases, though extreme, accentuated the vulnerability and the exploitation of female migrant workers.

As long as global economic inequalities exist, women will continue to migrate. For the community of practitioners, policy-makers, and academic researchers working on gender and development, this raises new issues. In particular, as the 'North' and 'South' take on a new configuration, since women from the Global South are struggling for their rights in communities of the North.

Worldwide, the number of women who migrate for employment purposes has dramatically risen in the last two decades, particularly in Asia — a phenomenon that has raised new issues and problems (Lim and Oishi, 1996). Attitudes towards the value of women's work have made their experiences as migrant workers different from those of

men, if not worse. The perception of domestic work as non-productive work that requires little skill has made women less likely to be protected by national legislation and institutions of receiving countries, as well as subject to provisions that are conducive to various forms of abuse. At the same time, women's migration has had profound social conse-quences in their home countries. Family separations and neglected children have been among the negative impacts of the phenomenon.

In the last decade, the majority of women who entered Canada to work as caregivers or nannies have been from the Philippines. Canada, on the other hand, has had a long history of procuring domestic workers externally. There have been numerous studies on the situation of domestic workers, but very few have been shaped or undertaken by domestic workers themselves. For the most part, they have been treated as objects of study, rather than agents of change. Over a six-month period in 1996, a group of 14 Filipina domestic workers carved time out of their busy lives to investigate and understand their working conditions and factors that gave rise to them, and more importantly, to identify action-oriented strategies to improve their situation. These domestic workers from Toronto and Montreal undertook the challenging task of learning participatory action research methods, identifying research questions, conducting focus groups discussions with other domestic workers, and presenting the findings.

The process

The goal of the project was to make the research as participatory and action-oriented as possible. A steering committee was established, which consisted of representatives of domestic workers organisations and collaborating organisations, namely the Women's Advisory Committee of the Philippines-Canada Human Resource Development Program (PCHRD), the Coalition for the Defence of Migrant Workers' Rights in Toronto, and PINAY in Montreal. These organisations set the goals of the project, and recruited researchers within and outside their respective organisations.

The first workshop
The first step in the research was to determine the research questions for the study. At the first workshop, participatory action research methods were introduced using both English and Tagalog. With the use of brainstorming, semi-structured interviewing, matrices, diagrams, trend analysis and historical profiles, a common understanding was achieved of the issues that shape the working and living conditions of domestic workers.

Within the group, there were different levels of awareness of the factors underpinning working conditions, and disagreement on the means to use to address them. As a result of these differences, the group was not unanimous on what the objectives of the study should be. Some wanted to address more immediate concerns, such as working hours, while others wanted to challenge the structures that perpetuate discrimination against migrant workers. Consensus, therefore, had to be carefully built, and eventually the entire group was able to select a research

theme: the conditions of live-in domestic workers. Research questions were then developed and agreed upon that would tackle three issues: immigration, employment and human rights, and family relations.

The second workshop
At the second workshop, the domestic workers were trained in participatory action research methods, using both English and Tagalog materials and learning exercises. With these skills, they would organise and facilitate focus groups of domestic workers themselves. Some of the principles of facilitation — such as avoiding lecturing, allowing everyone a voice, and not being threatened by disagreements — took time for members of the group to assimilate. Members saw conducting the research alone as a huge responsibility, and learning how to conduct the focus groups in a participatory way challenged people's former styles of forming groups and methods of research.

The research
A detailed research guide was developed, which outlined questions to be asked under each theme. Four research teams were formed, two per city, with four researchers on each team. The group also developed the criteria for the selection of focus group participants, and a timetable for the research and the sharing of results. The recruitment of focus group participants was guided by the principle of social diversity, and commitment to the research project. Domestic workers from varying age groups, social groups, and family backgrounds, who have different living and work arrangements, citizenship and employment status, and type of employer, were invited to participate.

With respect to the frequency of focus group meetings, a different approach was used in each city. In Montreal, six half-day focus group meetings were held over a two-month period. In Toronto, a single three-day intensive workshop was held. Historical profiling, trend analysis and semi-structured interviews were used to gather information. Researchers in each city worked as a core team, although they were subdivided into two research teams per city. They took turns facilitating and note-taking. After each focus group session, the teams analysed their results, and the weaknesses and strengths of the process.

Many of the researchers expressed a considerable amount of frustration with the research process at first. They had to listen to the problems and concerns of other domestic workers, yet they felt powerless to do anything to improve their situation. They didn't have the solutions being asked of them by the focus group participants. Some researchers acknowledged that they had thought that their own situations were bad, but after hearing about the situation of so many others, they considered themselves fortunate. By the end of the process, however, they acknowledged that both their experiences as researchers, and the insights that the study offered into their own lives, were extremely empowering. For many, the acquired participatory action research tools offered new ways of organising, confidence-building, and mobilising the domestic workers in their own communities.

In the following section, the results of the research on the realities of live-in domestic workers is presented, along with some of their personal testimonies.

The Findings

Living other people's lives: difficulties faced by workers within the household

'I feel frustrated and displaced. I had an office job in the Philippines, and for me to work in a house is something else'

Foreign domestic workers are required to live in the residence of their employers, and to have flexible working hours to suit their employers' way of life and requirements. They can be called upon at any time of the day to do virtually any type of chore, ranging from putting the children to sleep in the middle of the night, to walking the pets, to shovelling snow, to painting walls, to entertaining guests at midnight. As a result, it is difficult to draw the line between work hours and off-duty hours. Long working hours have, thus, characterised the lives of foreign domestic workers.

These long hours are often without financial compensation. In provinces where they are entitled to overtime, determining the magnitude of overtime work has been a challenge. What constitutes 'real work' depends on the attitude of the employer. For instance, the time spent by domestic workers waiting for their employers to come home late at night is not considered overtime by the employer, although it precludes other activities which domestic workers might want to spend their time on. Playing with children during off-hours may not be considered overtime, but it is difficult for domestic workers to avoid their employer's children, because they share the same living space.

Moreover, the peculiar status of domestic workers as non-standard workers and as non-family members has circumscribed their ability to assert their rights. For instance, gifts have created a relationship based on gratitude, and thus distract workers from the issue of wages and workloads. In some cases, domestic workers have been accused of stealing items that were given to them as gifts, when there is tension in the employer-employee relationship.

'Once when I was sick, my employer visited and I ended up babysitting her children..'

Unmonitored employment practices have put live-in domestic workers at a disadvantage. In instances when a caregiver has more than one employer, a practice known as the 'sharing of nannies', the workload is heavier without a corresponding increase in wages. This is an attractive option for employers who cannot afford to pay the full salary of a domestic worker. Another practice is to require a domestic worker to work without pay for a certain period, or a so-called trial period. This is illegal in Canada, but often domestic workers are forced into these arrangements, because they cannot remain unemployed for long periods of time. To do so jeopardises their opportunity to be eligible for landed immigrant status, as well as threatening their ability to survive financially.

Perhaps an issue of greater consequence is the curtailed lifestyle that comes with live-in work arrangements. In Canada, some live-in caregivers have been given substandard lodging facilities (for example, laundry rooms), and inadequate, or culturally insensitive, food. Although there are legal provisions with respect to the amount deductible from employees' salaries for room and board, there are no minimum standards set for food and accommodation to be provided by employers.

Lack of privacy, loneliness, and isolation are conditions that erode domestic workers' mental health. Domestic workers often do not have keys to their own rooms, or to their employer's house. There have been many instances when their right to privacy is not respected, with employers going through their personal belongings or having guests stay in the domestic worker's bedroom. There have also been cases when domestic workers are locked out of the employer's house when they do not come home at a designated time.

'I nurture feelings of hate, fear and stress'

Just as damaging to the self-esteem of domestic workers has been the practice of 'apartheid' (separate living defined by race). In many cases, due to cultural or racial prejudice, employers do not allow their domestic workers to share eating utensils, drinking glasses, toiletries, sheets and laundry facilities with their employers. While applicants in the Philippines are required to attend pre-departure training and orientation sessions, employers are not obliged to attend orientation sessions that would deepen their understanding of cross-cultural differences and their responsibility to respect the rights of domestic workers.

Living in the home of their employers has also made domestic workers prone to abuse. Many participants referred to experiences ranging from verbal abuse, to physical abuse from children when they do not get what they want, to sexual harassment. The private nature of the workplace conceals practices that are not acceptable in a regular work environment. It also makes it difficult to monitor and enforce labour standards or to ensure that contract violations do not occur.

In some cases, employers ask domestic workers to work in their businesses, in violation of the terms of the work permit. While refusal would mean the employer's displeasure, compliance could mean their deportation.

High costs, minimal returns?

'I can tolerate it because I am waiting for my papers'

Financial pressures further complicate the lives of foreign domestic workers. In the Philippines, applicants for overseas contract work bear onerous costs related to travel, recruitment, and government requirements. Some applicants pay exorbitant fees to recruitment agencies, which can be as high as US$3,500. The total cost of landing a job in Canada can be as high as C$8,300. Many migrant workers find themselves deep in debt early in the process.

Low economic returns and other difficulties faced by foreign domestic workers stem from the low value ascribed to domestic work. Historically, this type of work has been perceived as non-productive work that requires little or no skill. The integral relationship between domestic work and the functioning of the economy, and the role it plays in raising future generations, has been largely unrecognised (Folbre 1994). Despite a burgeoning demand for domestic workers as a result of women's contribution to the formal economy, little has been done in Canada or elsewhere to set up a universal and affordable child-care system. When provided in the formal economy, domestic work continues to be poorly remunerated.

As participants in this research confirmed, for many Filipina domestic workers in Canada, the promise of a better life has been soured by difficult living and working conditions, financial difficulties, and strained family relations. Moreover, the attainment of landed immigrant of citizenship status does not guarantee a good life. There are barriers to the upward mobility of domestic workers. While many were trained as teachers, nurses, accountants, and engineers, the educational background of foreign domestic workers is not recognised in Canada. Lengthy separations from their families have led to emotional stress, difficult parent-child relationships and family break-ups. The difficulties of re-adjustment upon family reunification, and family adaptation to a new culture, create yet another source of tension. Many family members are, in their turn, unable to find employment, or can find only low-wage jobs for which they are overqualified.

'Even after working for so many years, it seems like the income was only enough to support myself and pay bills'

Generally viewed as one of the best destinations for migrant workers, the researchers believe that Canada does not appear to live up to its reputation. While Canada may appear rosy compared to some countries in the Middle East, there is a lot more Canada can do to ensure the protection of the rights and well being of domestic workers within its borders.

Policy recommendations and action plan

After two months of participatory research, the researchers came together for a final gathering to share their results, summarise findings, and develop policy recommendations and an action plan for change to take back to their focus groups and organisations. Recommenda-tions were targeted at the Canadian govern-ment, the Philippines government, and the foreign domestic workers themselves.

Government policy changes needed in Canada

1 Abolish the Live-In Caregiver Program. Domestic workers should be recruited as independent immigrants, not linked to a particular employer.
2 Amnesty should be granted to domestic workers who came outside the formal recruitment program, who should be allowed to apply for landed immigrant status.
3 Implementation of immigration law should be standardised. Immigration officers should be consistent in processing papers.
4 The financial situation of domestic workers should be taken into account when setting fees for sponsorship, work permits, and applications for landed immigrant status.
5 Applications for landed immigrant status, renewal of work permit, etc, should be processed more quickly and applicants allowed to work while waiting for renewals.
6 Work permits should not be tied to a specific employer.
7 More points should be awarded to domestic work in applications for landed status, to reflect the true value of this work.
8 The policy of rejecting the whole family when one member is ineligible should be abolished.
9 Wages, working house, and benefits should be standardised, and workload clearly defined. The terms 'flexible hours' and 'flexible work-loads' should not be used in contracts. The provi-sions of the Employment Standards Act on worker entitlements (e.g. paid sick leave, accident insurance) should apply to domestic workers. Salaries should be increased, and the government should monitor working condi-tions. Workers should be allowed to study.
10 On arrival, domestic workers should be informed on their rights.
11 Live-in arrangements should not be mandatory.
12 Skills and educational background of domestic workers should be recognised, to promote labour mobility.
13 A regulating and collective bargaining body should be set up, comprising domestic workers, employers, and government. Its mandate should include the review of working conditions.
14 Employers should undergo orientation sessions to deepen their understanding of cultural differences, and awareness of their responsibility to respect the rights of domestic workers. There should be a mechanism to ensure their compliance with contract provisions.

Government policy changes needed in the Philippines

1 Regulations on recruitment agencies should be enforced. Agencies should be required to provide adequate information to job applicants before contracts are signed.

2 Fees for unnecessary services, requirements, or training courses should be abolished, to reduce the cost of applying for an overseas job. The processing of papers should be speeded up and simplified, to prevent corruption.

3 Orientation sessions for workers should provide more information about living and working conditions in destination countries.

4 The government should enter into a bilateral agreement with the Canadian government to protect Filipino migrant workers.

5 The government should focus on internal job creation, to reduce the pressure to migrate, and promote equality of rights for rich and poor.

Action plan for domestic workers in Canada
'The only healing part is when I joined organisations and got involved to help other domestic workers...'

1 Through educational activities in the Philippines, the belief that life is better in the West should be eliminated, and the myths about the lives of overseas contract workers exposed, to discourage migration. Workshops should be held for domestic workers in Canada to raise awareness of their rights. Cultural behaviour patterns such as 'debt of gratitude', shyness, and the impulse to co-operate at all costs, should be discouraged. Domestic workers should build their leadership and advocacy skills.

2 Transition houses should be set up for workers between employment, and support services established.

3 Existing organisations of domestic workers should be strengthened, and new ones formed, to meet the unmet needs of domestic workers. Unity among workers should be promoted, and regionalism and class discrimination discouraged. Workers should be involved in the process of social transformation in the Philippines.

4 Organisations of domestic workers should join national and international networks, and link with people's and women's groups in Canada and the Philippines.

5 Domestic workers should advocate for change through letter-writing to decision-makers, petitions, and awareness-campaigns.

6 The achievements of the project should be build on by training more domestic workers in participatory action research methods.

Conclusion

By examining the issues from the perspectives of domestic workers, the project has contributed to an understanding of the plight of women migrant workers. It has also been a learning and empowering experience for those who participated, some of whom have continued to conduct participatory research on their own. In Toronto, the Coalition for the Defence of Migrant Workers' Rights held another series of focus groups, in order to build on what was achieved in this participatory research project. In Montreal, PINAY project participants have continued their group-building activities.

This insight into the lives of Filipina domestic workers in Canada illustrates their struggles, not just for gender equality, but also for justice on the basis of race, class, and citizenship. Improvement of their lives will require, therefore, challenging the social and legal structures that maintain these inequalities. The participatory action research process, which enabled new strategic alliances amongst domestic workers, researchers and other social justice activists, is one step in that direction.

Nona Grandea, currently a Senior Policy Analyst at Status of Women Canada, was a Senior Researcher at The North-South Institute in Ottawa, Canada during the time of the project. Contact details: 360 Albert Street, Suite 700, Ottawa K1A 1C3, Canada. Fax: 00 613 947 0530, e-mail: grandean@swc-cfc.gc.ca

Joanna Kerr is a Senior Researcher at The North-South Institute. Contact details: 200-55 Murray Street, Ottawa, K1N 5M3, Canada. Fax: 00 613 241 7435, e-mail: jkerr@web.net

References

Folbre N *Who Pays for the Kids? Gender and the Structures of Constraint*, Routledge 1994

Lim, Lin Lean, and Oishi, Nana, *International Labour Migration of Asian Women: Distinctive Characteristics and Policy Concerns* ILO: Geneva, February, 1996

Gujurati migrants' search for modernity in Britain

Emma Crewe and Uma Kothari

In this article we consider international migration by drawing on the life stories of Gujaratis presently living in Wellingborough, to illustrate the varied and complex reasons for migration, and the contrasting experiences of men and women migrants.

'If people stay in one place there is no progress'

The stories were collected as part of a research project which was a response to some puzzling findings which emerged during earlier research by Uma Kothari in India in 1986–88. Despite their prosperity, farming households had family members living abroad either in the UK or East Africa, and those remaining had submitted visa applications and were waiting to migrate to Britain. Many of them had family and friends in Wellingborough, Northamptonshire, and were planning to join them. Why did an upwardly mobile group of people who were becoming such important and powerful actors in the South Gujarat agricultural scene choose to move to Britain where, like their family and friends before them, they would probably live in less favourable conditions?

This article asserts that many people from formerly-colonialised countries have migrated to Britain because they hoped that they would find a modern, civilised, and progressive place to live. For most, this search for 'modernity' in Britain has proved to be fruitless. In general, racism and unemployment, and perceptions of immorality and bad manners, have shattered their illusion of modernity in Britain. When Gandhi visited Britain and a journalist asked him what he thought of modern civilisation, he replied 'that would be a good idea'.

Understanding the complex causes of migration

Much migration and development studies literature has a preoccupation with the economic causes of migration. However, reasons for migration are in fact complex, and varied; many are non-economic (see Cohen 1997). This article challenges explanations that reduce reasons for migration to one cause, for example acquiring employment and wealth, and builds on discussions about migration, culture and identity (Hall 1992, Gilroy 1993). Instead of choosing between accounts which focus on individual motivation for migration, or explanations that look at global economics but ignore individuals, our research looked at migration from both micro- and macro-levels.

Following an introduction to the informants and the research methodologies, we examine the history of Gujarati migration to Britain, the experience and impact of moving and, finally, suggest how these issues are highly relevant to international development.

In this article we use a gender analysis as an essential tool for understanding migration processes. Relations between women and men shape and are shaped by migration (Wright 1995, Chant 1992). Until the mid-1970s, women were invisible in studies of migrancy, and when they did emerge tended to do so within the category of dependents of men, as Buijs (1993) argues. Much of the gender and migration literature concentrates on labour migration and labour markets or the distinct realm of employment in which men and women become involved following migration (Rowbotham and Mitter 1994). But we aim to go beyond a consideration of women's and men's different patterns of migration, to investigate individual women's and men's experiences of migration and the ways in which gender relations have been recreated and changed within and outside the household (see also Westwood 1988, 1995).

Methodology

From 1996–7, we interviewed Gujarati migrants in the town of Wellingborough. The most recent census tells us that the Wellingborough Gujarati community consists of approximately 2,300 people: just under 3 per cent of the population. The research was based on qualitative research methods; we collected people's life histories in semi-structured interviews at home, in their workplace, in community centres, shops, factories, and temple; or during community or religious meetings, events, and festivals. We also held a reminiscence group for elderly women living in sheltered housing. Finally we interviewed Pakistani, Afro-Caribbean, and white employers and community workers, and white residents living within a predominantly Gujarati residential area.

While people's descriptions of practices within the community could be analysed alongside the researchers' observation of those practices, interpreting the histories of migration was more complex. Life histories are objects of study in themselves rather than accounts of a progression of real events. They reveal as much about the present, the tellers, and listeners, as they do about the past.

When asking why they chose to migrate from one place to another, it became plain that people's memories were highly selective. Interpreting people's migration stories proved to be a process of analysing how memory is shaped by present social and cultural influences, as much as piecing together macro and micro factors affecting migration patterns. Similarly, when exploring who made decisions about migration, it was found that contradictions emerged within households. Claims about who made decisions appeared to reveal more about how power relationships are contested than how decisions were made in reality. For instance, the gendered nature of both collecting and interpreting life stories became obvious. Not only were experiences often divergent for women and men, but the revelations about their past were expressed very differently. Men tended to be less confiding and expose fewer emotional vulnerabilities than women, despite the stress they also experienced as migrants.

Another significant aspect of the methodology relates to the researchers' responsibility towards people who tell their stories. Throughout the research we wrote about it in community newspapers which are sent to every Gujarati household in Wellingborough. We also presented our findings in a booklet and a photographic exhibition for the Gujarati community.

Migration history of the Gujarati community

Migration to Africa began in ancient times when 400 girls from Gujarat were captured for the slave trade by Arab pirates. They were rescued but their families refused to take them back, so they were taken to Ethiopia. There the king found them 400 good Ethiopian boys to marry who allowed their wives to keep their own culture. Today, if you go to that place you will find the girls look like Indians. They are so beautiful that when any man sees them he feels that he will have to leave his wife immediately.

Above Arriving at Heathrow from Kenya in 1969

This is, according to a Gujarati teacher living in Wellingborough, how migration from India to Africa began. It reminds us that, for Gujarati women who, unlike men, nearly always move residence on marriage, migration from their parents' home is inevitable. The story also draws attention to the fact that if women's reputations are ruined, they can be forced into exile. Restriction on their mobility before marriage protects their own and their family's reputation, which is necessary not only for their own marriage prospects but those of other family members as well. It is already clear that gendered cultural rules and practices very directly shape migration.

Most Wellingborough Gujarati migrants are 'twice migrants' internationally, having first moved to East Africa after 1920 and then to Britain. Others moved directly from India to Britain from the middle of the 1950s. Initially, male migrants travelled on their own and returned to India every few years to visit

their family. It was men who sought employment while most women were not expected to find paid work in the public domain, and it was entirely appropriate for young men to set up a new residence on their own. There were, however, two women migrants who moved to Wellingborough independently. It is revealing that they had a history of refusing to conform to rules, both had left their husbands and, arguably, their reputations were already damaged by divorce.

Once financial security had been established, and residence in East Africa was seen as more permanent, women joined their husbands. The children of first generation East African Gujaratis often returned to India for education, more often than not with their mother accompanying them. During the Second World War, however, when it was virtually impossible to travel, children began to be educated through to secondary level in East Africa, and marriages were also arranged there, provided that a spouse of the right caste could be found (Dwyer 1994:180).

Gujarati migration from East Africa to Britain, mostly soon after African countries gained independence, varied quite considerably. Those who were forcibly exiled from Uganda by Amin in 1972 left in family groups. Those who had more time to plan, for example Kenya Gujaratis who knew in 1963 that they had to leave or take Kenyan citizenship within five years, often sent someone ahead to assess prospects in Britain. Irrespective of age, these 'scouts' were always male.

Agency and migration

Women are often represented as passive actors in migration, moving primarily at the command of a male member of the household. Either their motivation is not explored, or it is often supposed to be identical to that of their father or husband. Plainly, as Guy argues, some agents have more capacity than others to shape the process of migration (as cited by Wright 1995:781), but they are not always male. While it is true that the majority of Gujarati women we spoke to had migrated initially on marriage, it should not be assumed that migration is driven by men. First, to choose or agree to marry someone who has migrated is an affirmative decision, as decisive as choosing to move for any other reason. Furthermore, mothers and other female relatives were often involved in finding marriage partners.

Secondly, after marriage, twice- and thrice-migrant women often had an important role in deciding where to live. Some women we met claimed that they were the key decision-maker in deciding to move from one place to another. One Ugandan-born woman, for example, was so adamant that she did not want to live with her in-laws in Nairobi that she travelled to Kampala and remained in her parents' house until her husband was forced to join her. Many older men told us that they would like to return to India after retirement, but gave in to the wish of their wives to remain in Wellingborough to be near their children. Motivation in migration should not,

therefore, be associated only with men, because women can sometimes lead decision-making, and men and women may give different rationales for moving and for choosing one place rather than another.

Although a gendered perspective on migration is essential to understand the processes involved, the choices made by men and women also highlight certain patterns in common. Male and female life histories make it clear that individual material gain is an insufficient explanation for migration. For a great number of people, migration was involuntary (see also Cohen 1997). Those leaving East Africa were often compelled to migrate as a result of government policies. Others were under pressure if not compulsion. For example, men and women in India were persuaded to seek their fortunes or a good match in another country for the benefit of the family they were leaving behind. Thus, when there was a materially-based aspiration to this, it was meeting the interests of a much wider group than the individual.

Explanations for moving often called upon ideas about modernity; some said that they were hoping to 'progress' in a general rather than purely material sense. One Gujarati man was persuaded to move by his uncle who said 'if people stay in one place there is no progress.' Many women and men came to Britain, in particular, because they had high hopes of finding a modern, clean, 'civilised' country with high morals and plenty of opportunities. This is partly because 'ideas about Britain were largely derived from a colonial education system in which Britain was revered as the 'mother country' (Fryer 1984:374); and partly because relatives and friends depicted their experiences in Britain as more positive than they really were.

Many people spoke about the excitement of travel. As one informant put it 'Gujaratis have it in their blood to be enterprising, to migrate and to have a sense of adventure.' The idea of adventure, usually reserved for romantic tales about European explorers, plays a part in the story of Gujarati migration even if it is difficult to define.

The realities of living and working in 'modernity'

While some Gujaratis in Wellingborough are entirely satisfied with their life, the majority of women and men said that they were, on the whole, disappointed. Memories of East Africa focus on the time for leisure, the beautiful places and climate, and the active socialising and support between households; life in Britain, in contrast, is characterised as difficult. Many are saddened, for example, by its lack of zest. One man relates:

I spent my first night in a London hotel. When I looked out of the window at my usual rising time of 6 o'clock it was dark and deserted. In Tanzania it would be brightness and bustle at dawn so I assumed my watch was wrong and slept right through the morning. Then at last I realised that the liveliness I was waiting for would never appear.

The disillusionment for women and men tended to be different. Many women entered paid employment in Britain for the first time, mostly working in factories. Since their menfolk tend to be located in similarly disadvantaged positions, the income migrant women bring into the family often spells the difference between poverty and a fairly reasonable standard of living (Warrier 1988:134). Migrant women are still seen to be a cheap and flexible source of labour, and they continue to be over-represented in jobs that are characterised by low pay, low status, and little opportunity for advancement (Westwood 1988). Westwood has pointed out that when Gujarati women became wage earners it was, however, 'largely an extension of familial roles rather than a source of independence for women' (1988:120). Factory work meant no reduction in other household roles, such as childcare, supporting other households, and contributing to community projects (such as fundraising for Wellingborough's Hindu temple which was built in 1981).

Men had higher expectations than women of employment. Many were well-qualified when they arrived in Britain, but were discriminated against when looking for work and often failed to find employment appropriate to their qualifications and experience. In East Africa, in particular, many had had experience of managing people within the civil services, running small businesses or working for larger companies. When they could not find appropriate work in Britain, they often took factory jobs or remained unemployed. Although a large proportion, relative to the rest of Wellingborough's population, started businesses, many did so reluctantly and found running a small enterprise a struggle. As newspapers and almost all food products became available in supermarkets, many Gujarati-run businesses folded during the 1980s. Those that have survived depend on unpaid labour of other family members and chronic overwork on the part of all those involved. Men may have established most businesses in Wellingborough but, contrary to Westwood's findings (1988:121), their wives have often managed them because it would be too risky for both to give up paid employment.

Isolation and conflict

Contrary to the stereotype of harmonious, intensely supportive Asian 'communities', women often feel isolated and do not know who to turn to when suffering stress: One woman reported:

It looks rosy on the outside, but it's not always on the inside. It is difficult to get women to talk about their problems, they are in a trap. Some women get bullied and feel really isolated. Friends often do not want to get involved, and anyway they might gossip.

Women and men Gujaratis also relate to white people and other Gujaratis in Britain in different ways. Generational issues are as relevant as those of gender. For example, young women have greater restrictions on their behaviour imposed by their own relatives. Second-generation women are still custodians of moral values, and have to try to resolve tensions caused by different expectations. Peers from school or college want them to participate in youth culture by, for example, drinking and going to clubs. Parents, who often see white British culture as immoral and corrupting, try to constrain them and, in

18

Above A meeting at the Victoria Centre in Wellingborough to mark the anniversary of the founding of the Racial Equality Council

particular, regulate contact between young men and women. Young people employ brave and ingenious strategies to subvert their parents' aims, as one young women relates:

...the daughter will have promised to come back at 11 pm and then does not go home until 2 am. She faces her parents, she waits while they tell her off, and then it is all over. It was still worth lying in order to be able to go out... There are restrictions on clothes too. You can't expose your body, especially not your legs — but trousers are OK. If you do people say 'she's got no shame'. I would not wear a shoulder strap dress in front of my father, but I might go out with one under a shirt which covered everything and then expose the straps when I got to the club.

Young men are subjected to more physical racist violence than either older men or women. In common with other studies, we also found that while men expressed feelings related to unemployment, racism, and boredom (see Beliappa 1991), women's health problems were associated with isolation and conflicting expectations (see Fenton and Sadiq 1991).

Service provision for migrant communities
Mainstream services offer no appropriate, accessible and confidential way of helping either women or men with these problems. White-run statutory and voluntary organisa-

tions are failing in many other ways as well. In theory, all public services in Wellingborough are for the benefit of the whole population of the town including Black (Asian and Afro-Caribbean) people. Statutory authorities have tended to argue that the same needs exist within each community, and that all minorities should assimilate by using the same services as everyone else. But as one Gujarati commented, integration is not possible unless people are treated as equals. In practice, most government and voluntary agencies have been unable to ensure equality of access because their services are often inappropriate, hostile, and racist. As a result, members of Black communities are under represented as users of health and social care services (Wright 1993).

Given the shortage of opportunities in Wellingborough, many young people are moving to larger cities. Some Wellingborough Gujaratis have moved on to the USA or plan to do so in the future, and at least one has moved to India.

Conclusions: inequality and modernity

An explanation of migration is needed that integrates a gendered perspective, pays attention to political, economic, cultural and ideological factors, and places social processes within a historical and geographical context. Among Gujaratis in Northamptonshire, many different ideas had played a part in the decision to migrate, including ideas about how countries should modernise in imitation of the West,[1] images of 'home' versus the potentially utopian unknown lands, compulsion through family conflict, pressure from relatives, and government policy. In this list, culture and ideology are as significant as political and economic processes.

We have argued that a gender perspective illuminates our understanding of migration. The conditions, experiences, and impact of migration are inevitably gendered, in addition to being shaped by, for example, class, age, and caste. Since women's role in migration cannot be merely treated as an adjunct to men's, explanations that ignore the micro level (including gender relations) are insufficient.

Although gender relations shape and are shaped by migration, which inevitably leads to a complex explanation of processes, this does not mean we should retreat into an endlessly fractured and fragmented postmodern maze. Women and men may also share some motives and experiences of migration in common: for example, many have been searching for modernity in the context of colonialism, post-colonialism, and globalisation. The experience of Britain for the majority in Wellingborough has been disillusioning, and governmental, voluntary and 'community' support structures are inadequate. While Black community organisations require more resources to be effective, statutory agencies need to completely transform their policies and practices.

In particular, statutory agencies might, firstly, abandon the assumption that 'ethnic' minorities should assimilate. Critics have attacked this idea for decades, for example on the grounds that there is no unitary British culture to assimilate to, but the idea continues to thrive. Secondly, they need to recognise that different priorities, knowledge systems, cultural practices, and social inequalities exist between and within groups. Thirdly, they could improve accessibility to support services by, for example, making service counters more

welcoming so that all client groups are encouraged to use them. Fourthly, agencies need to take responsibility for combating racism, particularly at work, in public and private spaces, in education, and within the statutory agencies themselves. Statutory agencies need to acknowledge the problem of racism and work with Black groups to find appropriate solutions.

Some of these suggestions apply to agencies working in international development as well. There is an eerie silence about racism, for example, which urgently needs to be broken. Also, since their experience of Britain points to chronic social, economic and political problems within the country, the assumption that 'West is Best' should presumably be challenged. As Rattansi and Westwood point out 'Western modernity, however impressive its achievements, not only is incapable of providing solutions to basic problems of war and violence, environmental damage, economic exploitation, bureaucratic management and corruption, and equitable material comfort and security at national and global levels, but also chronically generates them as an almost inseparable part of its mode of operation' (1994:3).

Since the 1940s development practitioners from Britain have been travelling to so-called 'developing' countries to bring about modernisation through technology transfer, economic growth, and improved management (Crewe and Harrison, forthcoming). The idea of modernity embodies an irony which appears to have escaped the notice of many working in international development. We argue that development practitioners have much to learn from British Black people's experiences.

Emma Crewe is a researcher in the Department of Anthropology at University College London, Gower Street, London, WC1E 6BT, emma@crewster.demon.co.uk

Uma Kothari is a lecturer and researcher in development studies at the Institute for Development Policy and Management, University of Manchester, Crawford House, Oxford Road, Manchester M13 9GH. uma.kothari@man.ac.uk

Notes

1 We do not intend to emphasise the search for modernity above material factors as causes of migration.

References

Back, L (1996) *New Ethnicities and Urban Culture: Racism and Multiculture in Young Lives*, London: University College.

Bhachu, P (1993) 'Identities constructed and reconstructed: representations of Asian women in Britain', In (ed) G Buijs, *Migrant Women: Crossing Boundaries and Changing Identities*, Oxford: Berg.

Beliappa, K (1991) *Illness or Distress? Alternative Models of Mental Health*, London: Confederation of Indian Organisations.

Breman, J (1985) *Of Peasants, Migrants and Paupers*, Delhi: Oxford University Press.

Buijs, G (ed) (1993) *Migrant Women: Crossing Boundaries and Changing Identities*, Oxford: Berg.

Chant, C (1992) *Gender and Migration in Developing Countries*, London: Belhaven

Cohen, R (1997) *Global Diasporas*, London: University College.

Crewe, E and Harrison, E (forthcoming) *Whose Development? An Ethnography of Aid*, London: Zed.

Dwyer, R (1994) 'Caste, religion, and sect in Gujarat: followers of Vallabhacharya and Swarminarayan', in (ed) R Ballard, *Desh Pardesh: The South Asian presence in Britain*, London: Hurst and Company.

Fenton, S and Sadiq, A (1991) *Asian Women and Depression*, London: Commission for Racial Equality.

Fryer, P (1984) *Staying Power: The History of Black People in Britain*, London: Pluto.

Gilroy, P (1993) *The Black Atlantic: Modernity and Double Consciousness*, London: Verso.

Hall, S (1992) 'The question of cultural identity', in (eds) S Hall, D Held and T Mcgrew, *Modernity and its Futures*, Cambridge: Polity Press.

King, R (1995) 'Migrations, globalisations and place', in (eds) D Massey and P Jess, *A Place in the World*, Oxford: Oxford University Press.

Kothari, U (1997) 'Women's paid domestic work and rural transformation in India', in *Economic and Political Weekly* Vol.XXXII, No. 17, 1997

Potts, L (1990) *The World Labour Market: A History of Migration*, London: Zed

Rattansi, A and Westwood, S (1994) *Racism, Modernity and Identity: On the Western Front*, Cambridge: Polity Press.

Rowbotham, S and Mitter, S (eds) (1994) *Dignity and Daily Bread: New Forms of Economic Organising Among Poor Women in the Third World and the First*, London: Routledge.

Skeldon, R (1990) *Population Mobility in Developing Countries*, London: Belhaven.

Warrier, S (1988) 'Marriage, maternity, and female economic activity: Gujarati mothers in Britain', in S Westwood and P Bhachu, *Enterprising Women: Ethnicity, Economy, and Gender Relations*, London: Routledge.

Warrier, S (1994) 'Gujarati Prajapatis in London: family roles and sociability networks', in (ed) R Ballard, *Desh Pardesh: the South Asian presence in Britain*, London: Hurst.

Weiner, M (1990) 'Immigration: perspective from receiving countries', *Third World Quarterly*, 12(1), January 1990.

Westwood, S (1988) 'Workers and wives: continuities and discontinuities in the lives of Gujarati women', in S Westwood and P Bhachu, *Enterprising Women: Ethnicity, Economy, and Gender Relations*, London: Routledge.

Westwood, S (1995) 'Gendering diaspora: space, politics, and South Asian masculinities in Britain', in (ed) V van der Veer, *Nation and Migration: The Politics of Space in the South Asian Diaspora*, Pennsylvania: University of Pennsylvania Press.

Wright, C (1995) 'Gender awareness in migration theory: synthesising actor and structure in Southern Africa', in *Development and Change*, Volume 26 Number 4, October 1995.

Wright, R (1993) *Care in the Community: How it Affects Black Communities in Northamptonshire*, Social Services Issues Group.

Workers on the move:

seasonal migration and changing social relations in rural India

Ben Rogaly

This paper considers seasonal migration in different regions of India, and argues the need for a better understanding of social and economic relations and the circumstances under which migration can affect these to the benefit of poor migrant workers.

Seasonal and other temporary out-migration for manual work from Indian rural areas has been shown by many researchers to be a major component of the livelihoods of poor rural workers and their employers in most parts of the country (eg Racine, 1997 for south India; Breman, 1996 for western India). Men, women, and children moving around India in search of manual work pose a major challenge for develop-ment policy-makers. This is because, while seasonal wage workers are among the poorest people, they and their children are often excluded from geographically based interventions by their absence.

The number of temporary migrants has increased during the 1980s and 1990s in western India (Breman, 1996) and in eastern India (Ghosh and Sharma, 1995, p120). Mean-while, numbers of temporary migrants have 'not ebbed' in northern India (Srivastava, 1997, p23). National level estimates indicate that rural employment outmigration has 'probably' increased for India as a whole (Sen, 1997, p13). However, official information on the extent of seasonal outmigration is non-existent even at the local level, making

the planning of development interventions difficult. Thus, for example, it is not currently possible to determine either the most appropriate timing for rural employment pro-grammes or workable repayment schedules for micro-enterprise loans. In microfinance projects the collection of '[s]avings could be increase[d] by linking collection to the times and places of earning' (Mosse et al, 1997, p4).

The contention of this paper is that effect-ive policy and practice requires improved understanding of the extent, trends, causes, and consequences of seasonal migration. Seasonal migration is both a part of and an outcome of the structures[1] of social and economic relations in the Indian countryside. At the same time, through the actions of migrants and their employers, such migration can in some circumstances change those structures. In what follows, experiences of seasonal migration in different regions of India are contrasted. Based on the limited evidence available, hypotheses are suggested for further research into why there is a greater possibility of changing social relations through seasonal outmigration in some regions than in others.

Compulsion or choice? Contrasting two regions

The debate about whether women and men migrate seasonally because of structural preconditions (eg Shrestha, 1990), or whether it is a matter of individual choice is more complex than it might seem. Research in two regions of India referred to below illustrates how the economic factors determining why people migrate for work, and changes in these factors, vary according to the ways in which agricultural producer-capitalists organise themselves and their labour forces.

In general, the work migrants do, whether in agriculture, industry, construction or forestry, is mostly arduous, low-status, and badly paid. Manual workers in rural India are informally contracted, sometimes through intermediaries, and, like most rural workers worldwide, do not have effective collective bargaining mechanisms or legal protection from harsh employment practices (ILO, 1996). Teerink details the experience of Khandeshi migrants from Maharashtra, who are effectively compelled to migrate to work in sugar co-operatives in Gujarat (Teerink, 1995). They are deliberately excluded from local employment by employers seeking a cheaper, more pliable workforce. The organisation of sugar producers into a few very large co-operative processing plants, and the vertical integration of production (the processing plants manage the harvests) suggest the collusion of landowner-employers, acting together to successfully control their labour-forces, even though their businesses are not large-scale if taken individually (ibid).

For Khandeshi migrants, prior commitment to seasonal migrant work in the Gujarat sugar-harvest provides a means of subsistence, through the advances paid. Yet those same advances contribute to their indebtedness and dependency on employers. In contrast, many (though by no means all) seasonal migrant workers employed to harvest and transplant rice in West Bengal[2]

in eastern India, seem to experience a greater degree of choice.[3] Seasonal migration in West Bengal is not simply an inevitable part of the cycle of indebtedness, but can enable workers to save and even to accumulate capital on a very small scale.

Workers from the border regions of Bihar and West Bengal and from elsewhere in West Bengal have a long history of converging on the southern central part of the state for seasonal agricultural work. Since the increase in rice production in West Bengal in the 1980s and early 1990s, potential migrants have become aware that employment in transplanting and harvesting for a season is likely to be continuous (ie a month to six weeks for the same employer) rather than sporadic, and significantly better paid than working for employers in migrants' home areas. Migrants are paid a combination of a daily allowance of rice, accommodation and fuel, plus a lump sum of cash at the end of the season, and it has become common for migrants to return home with a lump sum of several hundred rupees (Rogaly, 1994). The predominantly small-holder owner-cultivators of south-central West Bengal do not collude to the same extent as sugar producers in the part of Gujarat studied by Teerink, but in contrast often act as rivals both economically, and in terms of relative social standing.

Changing economic and social structures: some connections

Rivalry for social status between local caste groups (referred to as *jati*) is particularly evident in West Bengal. Indeed, compared to elsewhere in the country, the status of particular *jati* in relation to others is relatively malleable (Davis, 1983; Basu, 1992). According to Basu's comparative study of women's organisations and class mobilisation among *adivasis*[4] in the Khandesh region of Maharashtra, and largely caste-Hindu[5] equivalents in West Bengal, social differentiation along the lines of class and caste was much more clear-cut (and thus less amenable to change) in the Maharashtra case (Basu op. cit.).

Connections between and changes in economic and social factors play a part in decisions (or compulsions) to seek employment as a manual worker. Gender ideologies, economic structures, and ideas about social rank interlink to influence decisions over which women and which men should do which kind of work, including manual work. Among caste-Hindus (and *dalits* — formerly untouchables — seeking to improve their rank by imitating caste-Hindu practices) in West Bengal, for women to be employed in manual work is considered a sign of very low status, with consequences for the rank of the whole *jati* in a particular locality. Many seasonal migrants in West Bengal are *adivasis*, among many of whom women's employment in manual work does not have such negative connotations. Yet ideology-based self-exclusion such as that practised in West Bengal by caste-Hindus and *dalit* women (which, if the work is arduous and low-paid, and if they in any case would have to hand over their wages, may be in some women's interests) shifts according to material circumstance: the poorer the household or wider social group, the less they can afford to exclude women from wage work, and the greater the likelihood that ideas about the status of wage work will be reoriented (Kapadia, 1994).[6]

However, such interactions between material conditions, ideologies of gender and caste, and engagement in wage work, are related to wider trends in the supply and demand for labour, and in the technologies associated with different forms of production. Moreover, these trends vary regionally. Migration into West Bengal is a consequence of seasonal shortages of workers, which are connected to technological change (i.e. rapid growth in groundwater irrigation), and exacerbated by negative ideas about the employment of local *dalit* and caste-Hindu women as wage workers (Rogaly, 1997b). Yet in Rayalseema District of Andhra

Pradesh in south India, men rather than women have withdrawn from the workforce as they increasingly find the terms of employment insulting compared to those they experienced earlier (Da Corta, 1997).

Structural causes of seasonal migration thus interact, and are also regionally differentiated. However, as we have seen, even this kind of migration, which is undertaken by some of the very poorest people, is not merely the outcome of structural conditions but contains, to a greater or lesser extent, an element of choice. The consequences of migration, which I will look at next, thus need to be considered not simply as what 'happens to' migrants and to social and economic relations, but also as the outcomes of migrants' deliberate actions.

Can seasonal migration change social relations to workers' advantage?

Seasonal migration has consequences for social and economic relations between several different categories of people:

- within and between migrant-worker households;
- between migrant workers and employers in source areas;
- between migrant workers and employers in destination areas;
- between local workers and employers of migrants in destination areas;
- between local workers and migrants in destination areas;
- between employers in source areas and employers in destination areas.

Despite sexual harassment, heavy workloads, and the adverse health consequences of poor living conditions, migration is not always the 'menace' (for the migrant workers concerned), that it is made out to be (eg in the Purulia District Plan, Government of West Bengal, 1991–92)[7]. Although I will illustrate this point by developing further the contrast between eastern and western India, others have argued that seasonal migration within a single context can simultaneously cause immense suffering and improve social relations from workers' perspectives (for example, Lenin, 1964, pp240–254).

The main contrast between my study of seasonal migration in West Bengal, and Teerink's in Maharashtra and Gujarat, is that in West Bengal social relations in the source areas showed greater potential to change to the advantage of the returning migrant workers and other manual wage-workers in the area. Employers in the Purulia locality, lacking irrigation, relied on a single rice crop. Most of the year they required very few paid workers; but for the transplanting (the exact timing of which depended on the start of the monsoon rains and was therefore relatively unpredictable) and for harvesting, they needed all the local workers they could get. Thus, employment opportunities in Purulia varied from periods when labour was urgently needed to periods when, as one worker put it, you just sat and watched the mosquitoes fly in front of your face. There was no seasonal in-migration. The two busy periods, transplanting in June-August and harvesting in October–December, coincided with increasing migration possibilities for local workers. Daily wages during harvest were a maximum of 12 rupees per day.[8]

There was little difference from the timing of the transplanting and harvest of one of the two main rice crops in Barddhaman District, where employers recruited migrant workers in response to seasonal shortages of labour and to help to control local workers' demands. Wages were approximately Rs 25 per day in the Barddhaman locality in 1991. Relations between workers and employers in Purulia changed as both the demand for migrant workers in Barddhaman and the level of real wages there increased. Employers, who had previously relied on historical obligations around provision of homestead land and annual subsistence loans, now had to change the way they addressed workers. In their turn, workers, confident in the knowledge of relatively well-paid work elsewhere, could be more assertive both in day-to-day dealings with patrons and in wage negotiations. In a neighbouring locality, an encounter between local employers and outsiders on a recruitment mission from Barddhaman District was laden with tension and violence. The visiting employers were instructed (by representatives of local employers) to leave the area immediately. The former had broken established caste ideologies by spending the night in the homes of low-caste workers and eating with them. Such changes, also entailing surprising cross-class alliances as well as fractiousness between members of the employer class, were indicative of wider progressive change from the Purulia workers' perspectives.

Migrants are also used by employers in the destination area to manage social relations with local workers. Migrants in the Barddhaman locality were given accommodation in outhouses in the employers' hamlets, thus remaining separate from local agricultural workers. They did not directly undercut local wages, which were based on a daily time-rate common to both men and women workers; in fact migrants' daily earnings were less bound by local institutional arrangements and in some cases exceeded those of local workers. It was the shared awareness by all parties of the relatively unlimited supply of migrant workers which strengthened the position of employers in wage negotiations with 'their' local workers.

Consequences for women and children

Sexual harassment

Women migrants have reported sexual harassment from employers,[9] contractors and — in the case of mixed migrant groups — male migrant workers (Banerjee, 1989-90). Most hiring and supervision of migrant workers, men and women, is carried out by men — either as contractors or employers.

Groups of migrants may be booked in advance if they have a history of working for a particular employer; may be sought out by employers or their agents combing known sources of migrant workers; or (increasingly common, according to available anecdotes) may seek work through negotiation at bus-stands and other evolving 'market places'. In West Bengal, migrants organise differently according to *jati*, with mixed-sex Santal[10] groups including just one member — who can be a man or a woman — from each household. Others, including other *adivasis*, form groups based on part- or whole-family units; in these cases, married women only travel if accompanied by their husbands. There is insufficient evidence to make a connection between the way the seasonal migration is organised and the extent of sexual harassment of women. However, it could be hypothesised that women having to spend one or more nights at labour market-places and travelling without kin, are more likely to be harassed by employers and contractors.

Reproductive work at the migrants' destination

In the West Bengal case, most of the reproductive work in groups of migrant workers, including meal preparation, is carried out by women. Women migrant workers thus maintain their additional workloads, which are particularly heavy where women travel with families, rather than in groups made up of one member from each of a number of families. In the latter case, migrants may select someone to be responsible for cooking for everybody (usually a woman) and negotiate for them to be let off work early each day. This would probably not be possible where there had been no previous relation with the employer concerned.

Can seasonal migration be liberating for women migrants?

It has been argued that seasonal migration can also be liberating for women migrants

in that they move away from restrictive social relations (inter- and intra-household) in source areas, and have greater autonomy as migrant workers (Thadani and Todaro, 1984). As Mosse et al (op cit) point out, however, whether women experience autonomy in migration depends on whom they travel with. For example, a young unmarried woman travelling in a group of cousins will have greater control over her earnings than similar women migrating with their fathers. The former are also likely to be motivated to migrate partly to experience 'the friendship and freedom of travelling with natal kin or a group of women their own age' (p41). Teerink concedes that *adivasi* women migrants 'are more free from social control than when they stay at their in-laws in the home village'. But she goes on to warn that drinking and smoking by *adivasi* women migrants did not necessarily indicate freedom and independence. They were 'still subject to male authority and patriarchy' (op. cit., pp250–251).

Effects on children and family disruption

Access to primary education is diminished when young children travel with their seasonally-migrant parents. '[S]easonal migration and illiteracy are narrowly intertwined. Young children who accompany their parents on the trek outside are destined to continue this type of roaming life at a later age' (Breman, op. cit., p48).In West Bengal, young girls accompany groups of migrants to care for infants, and are less likely to receive formal education than are boys.[11] Children in general are likely to suffer ill-effects from family disruption associated with seasonal migration in western India. 'Migration often aggravates existing tensions among and between men and women provoking conflicts, for example, between brothers competing for influence or fathers/uncles and sons/nephews' (Mosse et al, op cit, p41). The same study also gives seasonal migration as a cause of strained marital relations, sometimes as a result of new liaisons formed in migration destinations by both women and men, or if women who stay behind return to their natal homes in protest (p40).

Wages in arrears: employers' control mechanism or a useful means of saving?

Though not acting in combination in the same way as the sugar-processing co-operatives of western India described by Teerink, the employers of seasonally migrant workers in Barddhaman District sought other means of controlling their migrant workforce. Chief among these were provision of accommodation and payment in arrears. Although cash payments in arrears represented a form of saving for some workers, migrants could be faced with a stark choice between early departure and non-payment. In December 1991, the rice harvest in West Bengal was interrupted by five days of unseasonal heavy rain. Individual employers responded differently. Of the eleven migrants interviewed on their return to Purulia, nine reported employers withholding arrears payments in order to prevent the migrants returning home. Just two reported the continuation of the in-kind portion of payment during the rain.

To return home without wages caused great shame to one male worker, N, who had become ill during the rain (illness in the cold and wet conditions was not surprising given the inadequate accommodation available to migrant workers). N lived with his brother, A, who had a salaried job in the police force. The humiliation of not being able to bring home anything other than increased debt was hard for N to bear, and was directly attributable to his employer's failure to pay the wages owed.

I worked 18 days...The night it rained, I was there. I asked for the money, didn't get it. It was raining, he said I couldn't stay there. I had

some money and returned wet to the bus-stand at Barddhaman, came to Bankura and from Bankura I came back home at 10.30 at night. I returned to collect payment. I went to the employer's house. He said he'd send the money and rice through the hands of a man of my village. He didn't send it. Later he asked me to go again. Going is expensive. Return bus fare is 50 rupees. He turns me away every time. How can I spend so much on the bus fare — I haven't earned 50 paise.

Two women, J and B, from Purulia, were able to use remittances from seasonal migration to buy their way out of debt and tied employment relations, respectively. J had recently been widowed and left with two young children and a debt of Rs 400, against which her late husband's land had been mortgaged. Rs 150 was already owed in interest to the lender, a neighbour and fellow Bhumij. J migrated in November 1991 as part of a mixed-sex group of workers along with her young children, the youngest of which was being breastfed and accompanied J to work in the fields. On return J used remittances of Rs 325 to repay a large part of the loan and regain 0.75 bigha[12] of land. B, another Bhumij widow, had been a tied worker for the owner of the only rice-husking mill in the Purulia locality. She had been reliant on the regular employment to provide for her son and daughter. Now that her daughter was approaching puberty and thus eligible for employment in the fields, she calculated that together they would be able to survive long periods of scarce local employment by migrating seasonally. She left her employer and migrated with her daughter and dependent son in June 1991 for transplanting work. The Rs 450 and 20 kilograms of hulled rice she brought back lasted one and a half months, including expenditure on doctor's fees and repaying her debt to the grocer.

To the extent that some households can benefit financially and economically from seasonal migration, and that part of a woman's individual interests are associated with the wealth of the household of which she is a part, seasonal migration can be an opportunity for women as well as men. For example, a Bhumij married couple S, returned following harvest work in 1991–92 with Rs 900. Most of this was spent on a saree (Rs 200), petticoat (Rs 15) and trousers (Rs 150) for the forthcoming local *mela*[13], gambling (Rs 50), a goat (Rs 150), and gifts (Rs 50) for extended family and children. In this case, one consequence of seasonal migration was small-scale accumulation, probably to the benefit of both.

More research for improved policy and practice

It was intended that this article should make the case for more in-depth study of the interaction between seasonal migration and social relations, including gender relations, in rural India. Although there have been in-depth studies of seasonal migration, most notably those of Jan Breman in Gujarat over 30 years, there is a need for more systematic inter-regional comparison, as migration has different meanings, not just in terms of gender, class, and caste within a region, but between regions. These differences are probably related to different mechanisms for wealth accumulation used by agrarian and other capitalist producers.[14] However, more research needs to be done to examine this hypothesis.

Further studies might examine changes in different aspects of social relations within, as well as between, worker and employer households in source areas, on travel routes, and in destination areas. The outcome should be a move away from a 'one-size-fits-all' concept of seasonal migration on the part of policy makers, who have often portrayed it as a problem to be solved. Where, as in Purulia district of West Bengal, employers facing local labour shortages are able to bring disproportionate influence to bear on district planning agendas, such diagnoses may reflect particular class-interests. However, it is my contention here that blueprint project and policy responses to seasonal migration in India can partly be blamed on the lack of systematic comparative research on its differentiated causes and consequences.

Thanks to Manjari Chakravarti for help with transliteration of interviews; to Paramita Bhattacharyya and Khushi Dasgupta for assistance with fieldwork; and to the Economic and Social Research Council (UK) for funding.

Ben Rogaly is a lecturer in the School of Development Studies at the University of East Anglia, UK. He can be e-mailed on b.rogaly@uea.ac.uk or faxed on +44-1603-505262.

Notes

1 Structures refer here both to material factors such as the distribution of land-ownership and to ideologies, such as those associated with 'proper' behaviour for men and women, and for different castes. It is asserted in the text that such structures are not fixed but change over time, partly in response to the individual actions on which they also exert influence.

2 Research in West Bengal was carried out by the author between 1991 and 1993. This included nine months' intensive fieldwork in two localities, one characterised by irrigated double-cropping of rice, the other by rainfed rice production, in Barddhaman and Purulia districts respectively.

3 Albeit structurally embedded ones (see Rogaly, 1997a). Indeed, in an article based on recent research with migrant women in the same region, Rao and Rana (1997) argue that migration is a matter of compulsion here too because of diminishing possibilities for local livelihoods. In as much as Rao and Rana's findings diverge from my own, this illustrates the need to undertand *intra-* as well as inter-regional diversity. So far there is no comprehensive regional study of seasonal migration in eastern India. Rao and

Rana's study does not contradict my working hypothesis that agricultural employers in south Gujarat collude more successfully than agricultural employers in West Bengal and that, as a result, migrant workers moving into West Bengal agriculture experience a greater degree of choice than those in south Gujarat.

4 lit. original inhabitants, often referred to as 'tribals' in official discourse

5 'Caste-Hindu' is used here to refer to all Hindus other than the formerly 'untouchable' *dalits* (lit. oppressed people; 'scheduled castes' in official parlance).

6 Kapadia's research with women and men rural workers is based in Tamil Nadu in south India, where gender and caste ideologies differ from those in both the regions discussed here. However, Kapadia's general point about the interrelation between ideologies and material circumstances is supported by the West Bengal evidence.

7 I have argued elsewhere that such policy documents may reflect the interests of dominant agrarian classes seeking to protect their supply of workers (Rogaly, 1994).

8 Worth approximately two kilograms of hulled rice at the time of field research

9 Sexual harassment of women workers by male employers can be seen as a reflection of the combined power of the latter as men and as payers of wages.

10 The Santal tribe make up the largest number of seasonal migrant workers into Barddhaman District (Rao and Rana, 1997, p3188).

11 Rao and Rana found very low attendance levels for both boys and girls in the migrant source area they studied. However, girls' attendance was even lower than that of boys (op cit).

12 There are three *bighas* in one acre.

13 Fair.

14 Much seasonal rural outmigration in western India is to work in construction and industry (Breman, op cit; Mosse et al, op cit).

References

Banerjee, Narayana, 1989–90, *Family Postures vs Family Reality: Strategies for Survival and Mobility*, Samya Shakti, (IV and V).

Basu, Amrita, 1992, *Two Faces of Protest: Contrasting Modes of Women's Activism in India*, Berkeley: University of California Press.

Breman, Jan, 1996, *Footloose Labour: Working in India's Informal Economy*, Cambridge: CUP.

Da Corta, Lucia and Venkatesh Venkateshwarlu, 1997, 'Labour Relations, Domestic Relations and the Feminisation of Agricultural Labour in Andhra Pradesh', paper presented at a Workshop on Rural Labour Relations in India, London School of Economics, June.

Davis, Marvin, 1983, *Rank and Rivalry: The Politics of Inequality in Rural West Bengal*, Cambridge: CUP.

Ghosh, P.P and Alokh N. Sharma, 1995, 'Seasonal migration of rural labour in Bihar', *Labour and Development*, 1 (1).

ILO, 1996, *Wage Workers in Agriculture: Conditions of Employment and Work*, Geneva: International Labour Office.

Kapadia, Karin, 1994, 'Gender in Rural Industry in South India: Family Income, Expenditure and Responsibility in the Household', draft workshop paper.

Lenin, V.I., 1964, *The Development of Capitalism in Russia, Collected Works, Vol iii* (2nd Edition), Moscow: Progress Publishers.

Mosse, D., S. Gupta, M. Mehta, V. Shah and J. Rees with the KRIBP team, 1997, 'Seasonal Labour Migration in Tribal (Bhil) Western India', Draft Preliminary Report, Swansea: Centre for Development Studies.

Racine, J., 1997, *Peasant Moorings: Village Ties and Mobility Rationales in South India*, New Delhi/Thousand Oaks/London: Sage.

Rao, Nitya and Kumar Rana, 1997, 'Womens' labour and migration: the case of the Santhals', *Economic and Political Weekly*, 32 (50).

Rogaly, Ben, 1994, 'Rural Labour Arrangements in West Bengal, India', unpublished DPhil thesis, University of Oxford.

Rogaly, Ben, 1997a, 'Embedded markets: hired labour arrangements in West Bengal agriculture', *Oxford Development Studies*, 25 (2).

Rogaly, Ben, 1997b, 'Linking home and market: towards a gendered analysis of changing labour relations in rural West Bengal', *IDS Bulletin*, 28 (3).

Sen, Abhijit, 1997, 'Recent Trends in Employment, Wages and Poverty in Rural India', paper presented at a Workshop on Rural Labour Relations in India, London School of Economics, June.

Shreshta, N.R., 1990, *Landlessness and Migration in Nepal*, Boulder: Westview.

Srivastava, Ravi, 1997, 'Rural Labour in Uttar Pradesh: Emerging Features of Subsistence, Contradiction and Resistance', paper presented at a Workshop on Rural Labour Relations in India, London School of Economics, June.

Teerink, Rensje, 1995, 'Migration and its impact on Khandeshi women in the sugar cane harvest', in Loes Schenk-Sanbergen (ed), *Women and Seasonal Migration*, New Delhi: Sage.

Thadani, V. and M. Todaro, 1984, 'Female migration: a conceptual framework', in J. Fawcett et al (eds), *Women in the Cities of Asia: Migration and Urban Adaptation*, Boulder: Westview.

Below The labour-intensive work of transplanting rice seedlings provides seasonal employment for migrant workers in many parts of India.

R Shaw/Oxfam

Food shortages and gender relations in Ikafe settlement, Uganda

Lina Payne

Migrating to another country, and settling there as refugees, has practical implications for the lives of men and women, and for social relations. Women face social vulnerability as a result of changed gender relations, despite opportunities to challenge existing stereotypes concerning women's and men's roles and identities. This article describes the coping strategies adopted by Sudanese refugees in Ikafe, Uganda, and the effect of these on social relations, and suggests policy changes that could alleviate the situation.

Between 1994 and 1997, Ikafe settlement in Arua District, northern Uganda, accommodated around 55,000 refugees from Southern Sudan. The long-term objective of the relief programme was to move towards self-reliance for refugees. People were settled in small dispersed communities and given opportunities to cultivate crops and develop livelihood stragegies. In the interim, full food rations were donated by the World Food Programme (WFP), and Oxfam GB (formerly, Oxfam UK and Ireland) was responsible for distribution. A year and a half after its inception, the whole programme was disrupted by violent activity by Ugandan rebels, which affected the area for much of 1996 and into the early part of 1997. Thousands of refugees were displaced from their homes and agricultural land during a period of about six months from October 1996 — at the same time that food rations were delayed because of rebel action on the road from Kampala. By March 1997, virtually the whole population had migrated first to other less disturbed points, then into 'protected' transit areas within the settlement of Ikafe, and when those were attacked, to nearby towns.

During this period, the majority of families lost any independent source of livelihood, as they were unable to reach their fields to harvest crops, businesses failed, and markets that had begun to flourish within the settlement collapsed. Refugees once again became reliant on outsiders to provide food and other basic necessities — at a time when food supplies were delayed and other resources generally limited. They were forced to adopt a series of short-term coping strategies to deal with the situation.

The changes outlined here were observed over a period of a year, as refugees coped with fluctuating levels of insecurity and food shortages as a result of the violence. Oxfam employed two full-time social researchers on the Ikafe programme, who were responsible for the collection and analysis of information for use in programme planning and monitoring. They worked closely with a team of 15 refugee extension staff, men and women with various sectoral specialisations, who represented the different tribes making up the settlement. These staff were given training in the use of PRA tools and data analysis. Information was collected throughout the period of insecurity, mostly using small group or individual semi-structured interviews. People tended to have difficulty thinking beyond the expected imminent attack, and groups were reluctant to gather together. A number of informal workshops were held with the team and some key people from within the community to discuss and analyse the data. All the quotations in this article come from these discussions.

Coping strategies

Harvesting in unsafe conditions
People continued to monitor the state of their crops from a distance, through informal networks among both refugees and local Ugandans, or by returning to their fields on foot — a distance of 5-12 kms along extremely unsafe routes. Harvesting food crops became a priority, except for a very few of the refugees who had other sources of income.

Women are normally responsible for harvesting, but it was usually men who risked the journey, especially after a series of rapes of women who had left the relative security of the camps. Single women did not usually have any choice but to risk travelling the roads alone. 'The most movement is the harvest movement. The young girls and women fear much because of the raping. But conditions force them to go to their fields to harvest their crops' one woman explained when she was displaced to a large transit area within the settlement. Men, mostly travelling alone, were at risk of beating, looting, and killing. A number of refugees of both sexes were abducted by the rebels and taken across the borders for training, or to be used for sex.

Even before the rebel activity, some families were forced to harvest their crops prematurely because of food shortages. In many cases, entire seed crops were sold or exchanged at very poor rates of exchange.

Employment in 'leja-leja'
Wherever possible, refugees sought piece work *(leja-leja)* through local people, mostly agricultural work, digging, weeding or harvesting. Wages tended to be highly exploitative, because of the fierce competition for work throughout the settlement, and became more so with the increased number of displaced refugees who could not get to their own plots and were therefore reliant on cash income.

Culturally ascribed gender roles are more or less similar for refugees and local people. The two cultures are historically closely aligned, and a number of tribes cross borders. In the context of Ikafe, this limited the choice of work available to men in particular: while digging was done by men and women, weeding and harvesting were mostly available only to women. The fact that women then were more likely to be able to earn some income was felt particularly hard because rebel activity reached a height during the long harvesting season.

Men had already lost economic and social status as a result of becoming refugees in Ikafe, particularly as there were few opportunities for off-farm activities traditionally carried out by men, such as business or trading. This was coupled with the breakdown of traditional community and kinship systems in which men played a more prominent role. Allied to loss of status was a sense of powerlessness in the face of the insecurity. Respondents often reported that there was more apathy among men. Women were more prepared to go in search of wild food in the bush, or to accept lower rates of pay in the highly competitive job market. They often became the major income providers for the household.

Sexual exchange as a survival strategy
Before the insecurity, there was little for men to do to support the household other than farming, but even then, plots were

smaller than people had been used to in Sudan. As they found the man in the home unable to perform the expected role of providing for the household, some women abandoned their families (and sometimes their communities) to stay as 'wives' with local men who had better access to food and other assets. A few unmarried and young girls became involved in selling sex more directly.

Depletion of assets

Other options were limited. Small-scale business threw refugees into a vicious circle once food rations were delayed, as profit from activities such as brewing or petty trading were used to buy food, instead of being re-invested. Fewer and fewer small-scale businesses were sustained; cash was generally short, and markets collapsed. Meanwhile, petty theft increased. Food products with high nutritional value, such as *simsim*, which is a good source of protein, tended to get exchanged for more staple food-stuffs, especially maize flour. Some families sold off any remaining assets in order to buy food. 'How can you let a small children go hungry when you still have a cooking pot or some clothes sitting beside you?'

Practical implications of the crisis

Problems facing single women and men

Informal support mechanisms had tended to be weak in Ikafe, where a dislocated population had been thrown together in a situation where they were rarely able to make traditional claims upon each other. Once the settlement was disrupted by violence, communities were even more disoriented, and ties of responsibility to those close at hand broke down still further. Tribal networks that cut across the settlement became more prominent; ethnic groups tended to look to themselves first. 'People from one tribe move together to look for *leja-leja*, and they keep each other informed of oppor-

tunities and movements', a woman from the minority Avokaya tribe complained.

Single people, especially those from minority tribes, were more isolated, and single men and women with young dependents were particularly vulnerable. 'Women without men are suffering the most', one refugee explained in a personal communication at the time. 'Men move all their women, children and property to the bush. Single women get left out. Some have left properties because they could not carry them.' This was noted at a time when the number of single women within the settlement had actually increased as men returned to Sudan in search of food, to fight, or to attempt to cultivate land in preparation for a full-scale return.

Single women were more likely to enter unwanted marriages or get involved in other socially unacceptable activities as survival strategies, including selling or bartering sex — which affected their position within their own society. While they were able to ensure that their practical and welfare needs were being met, at the same time they became economically dependent on someone else, and often lost sources of liveliood and essential support mechanisms within their own communities. During two workshops held with refugees to discuss the implications of the overall insecurity, a number of people mentioned cases of girls who had stayed with soldiers in Ikafe and had been forced to leave their parental homes for good, when they were not accepted back into the community after the military presence was reduced.

Exchanging domestic roles

Where families stayed together, women very often became the primary providers for the family. Sometimes (but certainly not always) men took on some of the reproductive reponsibilities, especially cooking and caring for children. It often fell on them to collect firewood and grinding stones, or queue for water — all traditionally 'female' tasks — particularly at night, because they were afraid for women to move far beyond the transit camps with the ever-present risk of rape.

Decline in health

Apart from the social and economic concerns, cases of malnutrition increased considerably as the area became more insecure. Old people and young children were particularly vulnerable to sickness, but even those normally capable of walking a long distance or working a full day were less able to do so once they were weakened by hunger. Women who had been raped as they went in search of food, or when cultivating land in insecure areas, needed immediate medical attention. This was rarely available, because health centres had been heavily looted and most of the qualified staff had left. Many women were too ashamed to go: 'I didn't go to the clinic because of the shame. It's better to just keep quiet and try to get over it alone', a woman from Ikafe explained. Women who had increased their number of sexual relationships as a survival strategy increased their vulnerability to contracting HIV/AIDS and other sexually transmitted diseases, as well as risking pregnancy.

People already faced enormous mental strain every day, as they struggled to meet the food needs of their families. Yet there were few support mechanisms, especially to help men and women to deal with the trauma of violence. Traditional healing and other support mechanisms, including the church, elders or close relatives, were no longer functioning in the refugee context. People were left to cope alone. Everybody was suffering the violence of the rebel attacks, and this may well have detracted from the specific emotional needs of both men and women. All those who had been raped spoke of an enormous sense of shame; some were afraid to move out beyond the immediate environment of their homes; many were demoralised and demotivated and had lost interest in managing their affairs, which made them even more vulnerable.

Changes to gender relations in the household

Impact of changes in sexual division of labour

As women took on the role of going daily in search of food, their work burdens, as well as the psychological pressures upon them, were increased. Many lamented the loss of support: 'He is no longer like the man in the house', a woman refugee complained of her husband. Yet recognising changes in the sexual division of responsibilities did not extend to a more strategic questioning of traditional concepts of women and men's work. In the few households where men had taken on domestic chores, respondents noted only that men's sense of inadequacy had grown, as they felt the pressure to assume women's roles: 'Doing women's work makes them feel bad about themselves.' It was not uncommon for men to start drinking more heavily, which in turn affected women, who suffered as men voiced frustrations or attempted to reassert their authority through violence.

Changes in decision-making

There was no evidence that the practical changes led to very great changes in women's and men's power to make decisions. There were cases where women did suggest that they had gained power since taking more responsibility for food provision. Two women interviewed in February 1997 for example explained how: 'women are doing the men's work now ... It is women who are making the decisions.' However, women's sense of having more power and input into decision-making was probably more perceived than actual. 'Even if a woman still has budget, he can still take it and she will get only a beating', one woman explained. And women were still suffering from preferential feeding habits of men and male children, which our research indicated continued in Ikafe. In

34

polygamous households, for example, men continued to eat food prepared by each of their wives.

Increased domestic quarrelling

Most people interviewed during the long period of insecurity said that the majority of domestic arguments revolved around the need for food. As one respondent put it: 'Most problems are because of hunger. A woman goes for *leja-leja*. Immediately she returns home, her husband asks her for something to eat. But the woman has not had any time to prepare anything. Then she finds there is nothing to cook for sauce. When the man asks why not, of course she will reply: "You know it's you to provide it", and the fighting breaks out.'

There were also more domestic arguments as a result of the changes in gender roles outlined above, which brought changes in the control men and women had over food. As men took on harvesting, they began to take decisions about sale, storage and consumption of crops and food, which had previously been made jointly. Women respondents suggested they had lost the capacity to make what they saw as more strategic decisions related to food. 'A man, if he has got money today, will waste it on

local beer and cigarettes', one woman pointed out. 'If a man or woman sells food unnecessarily, it brings conflict.' Women in particular spoke of an impact on the health status of the entire family as a result of these changes in the sexual division of labour.

Marital break-down

Women who had already been raped as a result of their efforts to ensure family survival faced the likelihood of rejection by their own families. They typically complained of more domestic quarrels, and a few were abandoned by their husbands. 'Her husband left her when he discovered she had been raped by three men; it was the shame and the fear of AIDS' one woman refugee explained.

Some respondents asserted that marital break-down happened because women were too tired to have sex at night.'This confusion is making a lot of women leave their husbands. Families are breaking up because food is not there ... the women are too tired [to perform their responsibilities] and fighting breaks out. This is all because of hunger', a woman refugee and member of the Refugee Council (the main refugee political and administrative body which represented the whole settlement) explained. Some women chose to return to the homes

Right
Food distribution,
Ikafe settlement.

Jenny Matthews/Oxfam

of their refugee parents where they felt more confident that their food needs would be met.

Simply knowing that there was a commitment from outside to meeting food needs for the medium term gave some women a new-found freedom. Since security and food supplies have improved, there have been cases of women leaving husbands who had previously been beating them. This ability to move out is frequently put down to the fact that UNHCR has now become like 'the man of the house'. As a woman Chief explained: 'even if I had a man, if he argues, I would say "My husband is UNHCR now. He is the one to provide everything."'

Changes to gender relations at community level

The changes in gender roles and relations at household level had an impact on people's participation in community activities. Some men lost confidence, and felt a growing sense of powerlessness, which was compounded by their having to take on women's roles. As some men withdrew from earlier responsibilities within the community, women often took their places.

In addition, a significant number of men chose to leave the settlement and return to Sudan following SPLA (Sudanese People's Liberation Army) advances in early 1996. Their return was often put down to the stresses of food shortages: many claimed to have gone in search of food or to prepare land for the next season. Their departure brought some *de facto* changes in refugee representation within the settlement, and women sometimes took on that role.

Implications for policy

This article has looked at the changes in gender roles and relations resulting from displacement. Much of the focus has been on issues of food security, because it was the inability to meet their basic food needs

that was a priority concern for refugees at the time, and that forced the debilitating coping strategies the article describes.

How people reacted and the choices they were forced to make depended on a whole range of factors, among them kinship structures, external (and cross-border) support, levels of education, previous experiences; and as much as anything, on personality. Yet ultimately the practical choices related to the ability or inability to obtain food.

Helping refugees to cultivate wherever possible was an important way of reducing future vulnerability in Ikafe. Refugees asked for seeds even at the height of the violence. Many approached local farmers to lend them land. Providing seeds even in quite desperate situations can bring a sense of stability, and provides some future security.

Below Clearing ground preparatory to planting a food crop in Ikafe, before violence and insecurity forced people to abandon this plot.

Jenny Matthews/Oxfam

Access to any form of income (or food) became crucial for present and future security. Markets collapsed in the wake of the violence, but not entirely. Women were still seen brewing in the transit areas, which meant that a cash economy of sorts continued to operate. Men in particular asked for small loans for petty trading and to redevelop skills-based trades. In Imvepi, a neighbouring camp to Ikafe, Oxfam has explored a system of giving out very small loans with a fast repayment schedule of just three months. These are paid out directly to individuals, as a quick way of stimulating business within an unstable environment. They are relatively low risk, and so far the repayment rate has been over 90 per cent. Refugees speak very highly of this loan system: 'It gave me the opportunity to restart my blacksmith business in the transit camp at a very important time. People needed things welded and new cooking pots more than ever after all the troubles'(personal communication 1997).

In Ikafe, we looked for opportunities linked to other programmes, such as making saucepan lids for improved environmental practice; and production of scoops for food distribution. But it was little more than a drop in the ocean. Another avenue is to support some of the more positive coping mechanisms, like offering seed banks to give a assistance against distress sales when market prices are deflated.

Where food supplies are under threat, buffer stocks can provide some security; agencies could also consider local procurement of food in order to pre-empt sales of assets. Another option is to look at replacing non-food items sold locally. Providing food rations retrospectively may allow refugees to recover items pawned or sold, and to repay debts, but it could also have a negative impact on market prices and local

production systems as food is sold off to recover a household's assets.

Helping men to reassume the role of provider by enhancing opportunities for them to earn income or obtain food not only takes the pressure from women, it also enables men to win back some social and economic status, and with it perhaps some of their motivation — as well as providing much needed food. In Ikafe, Oxfam tried to look for other opportunities to support some of the less tangible socio-political implications of displacement that have been outlined in this article. Research was initiated into traditional healing mechanisms and to identify key people within the community to work through. Support was given to rebuild cultural activities to bring a sense of community back to the displaced population. Elders and chiefs were helped to make tribal drums which are used in various ceremonies and worship; and footballs and volleyballs were provided for the young people.

It is especially important for displaced societies to rebuild community networks, because traditional social values have often broken down. In this article, we have seen how women resorted to survival strategies that jeopardised their longer-term security: selling or bartering sex, in particular. Focusing on short-term tangible inputs can help to bring a sense of cohesion to a very unstable and unsupportive community environment, which in turn will help people to cope with the pressures of day-to-day living at a time of food crisis.

Lina Payne worked as a social researcher on the Ikafe programme. She is the author of the forthcoming book on Ikafe, to be published by Oxfam in 1998. She is now a social policy consultant. She can be contacted via The Editor, Gender and Development.

Mental illness and social stigma: experiences in a Pakistani community in the UK

Erica L. Wheeler

Through an examination of the role of women in the family, and concepts of mental illness within the Pakistani community and the British context, this article discusses the reasons why the experiences of hospitalisation and subsequent treatment with drug therapy in the community is so stigmatising for Pakistani women.

In writing this article, I have drawn on research with a wide focus, using a sample of patients[1] previously discharged from in-patient psychiatric care, approximately two-thirds of whom are migrants from Pakistan and the remaining one-third first-generation Britons, to discuss some adverse and unintended consequences of psychiatric care on Pakistani women resident in West Yorkshire.

The hospitalisation of Pakistani women who participated in my research has had an adverse effect on their role and social standing both within their family and the wider community. Research on community mental health among Asians by Beliappa (1991) in the south of England has shown that 92 per cent of people who saw their roles as negated, experienced distress. This distress could result from conflicts in the family; damage to women's roles and responsibilities; and sometimes the removal of the support from extended family and associates that women have formerly received.[2] The article highlights the implications of current

psychiatric treatment, and makes some recommendations for policy-makers.

The family, gender, and ties to *biraderi*

Among women in my research sample, the roles (and the concomitant obligations) most severely affected by a diagnosis and treatment of mental illness are those of wife and mother, which form the core of women's identity within the family. When Haleh Afshar (1994) researched attitudes to education and employment among Muslim women in West Yorkshire (some of whom had come from Pakistan), she acknowledged her surprise that marriage and motherhood were often seen by women as being more important than either of the topics which her research set out to look at. This view is in harmony with sentiments expressed by Quddus, a Pakistani author commenting on roles within the family:

the family still retains its pre-eminence in Pakistan as the strongest bond of association ...The father is the breadwinner and the mother runs the home. This demarcation works for harmony (Quddus, 1995: 73).

The organisation of families along patrilineal lines, the distance separating women from their families of origin through international migration, and the fact that most women do not go out to work, has led to a constriction of opportunities for social interaction, especially among middle-aged and older women. Khan describes Mirpuris from the Azad Kashmir region of Pakistan (who were included in this research) as 'probably among the most encapsulated and home-orientated of Asian migrants to Britain' (Khan, 1979:38).

The roles, responsibilities, and expectations within the extended family may extend not only to family members in the local environment, but to relations in Pakistan as well. In addition, beyond the nuclear and extended family, as pointed out by Anwar and Khan, there are also wider obligations to the *biraderi*. This is a Pakistani Punjabi term meaning a 'brotherhood' based on descent from a common male ancestor. Belonging to a *biraderi* is said to give a strong sense of psychological security and 'functions as a welfare, banking and advice service' (Khan, 1979:45). In addition, the *biraderi* performs a role which is important in the context of this discussion: that of 'psychiatrist' (Ahmad 1996, referring to Wakil 1970).

Seeking help from traditional sources

Fernando (1991) argues that many Asian groups do not differentiate between culture, religion, medicine, and ethics in the same way as Western cultures do. Furthermore, there is no sharp distinction made between 'illnesses' of the mind and of the body. It is therefore quite acceptable for an Asian to visit a traditional healer whose spiritual or religious approach is considered appropriate for resolving their emotional problems or distress; visits to

such a healer or 'holy man' do not attract stigma. There was some evidence, though limited and possibly under-reported, that spouses took women to visit holy men or *hakims*. Rack (1982) points out many African, Asian, and African-Caribbean people in their countries of origin would not go to a psychiatrist unless they were indeed 'mad'.[3] A mental hospital is therefore seen as a place of last resort.

For members of a migrant community, it is not always possible to seek support from the extended family or *biraderi*. One woman, speaking of the need for support said:

...at times like that sometimes I wish I had a mother or a brother or a sister in this country where I could go and off-load myself.

There is a recognition that the stresses of separation brought about by migration, and other factors such as bereavement, contribute to emotional distress, and that with support from the family they might have been able to cope. The informant quoted above, who lives in a nuclear family, and whose husband had himself been in and out of mental hospital over many years, said:

This is why I developed all these worries and all this stress, keeping all these things inside, and on top of it my husband beating me up and shouting at me, and I didn't get any support from anybody, from relatives or friends. I haven't got anybody of my own in this country who would give me support and help.

Respondents' views of the causes of their health problems

Many women clearly identified the outside causes of their health problems as family problems, traumas, or conflicts. Such problems were also described by Asian women talking about the sources of their depression in other research (Fenton and Sadiq, 1993). Terms such as *parishani* (worries) or *takleef* (emotional problems) were acceptable to women and to their families as descriptions of their distress, because they were seen as natural responses to external stresses and problems. Women saw themselves as 'under pressure' from their *takleef* which gave rise to an illness of the mind, *deemag bemari*, but not as suffering from a pathological illness or 'madness'.

There are no direct translations of psychiatric terms such as 'depression' or 'schizophrenia' into Urdu/Punjabi or Mirpuri (the most common languages spoken by informants). However, the word 'mental' is translated as *'pagal'*: literally, 'a lunatic', a 'mad', or 'crazy' person . The term does not appear to allow for different degrees or types of 'madness' (such as depression, which is seen in psychiatry, and by the public, as a less severe or dangerous form of illness compared to schizophrenia). The fact that a doctor admitted an individual to a mental hospital meant a shift in perception from being *deemag bemari* to being *pagal*, with its connotations of permanence and stigma.

A majority of the informants indicated that use of this term is unidimensional and negative:

...well, if you say mental, if you translate anything mental, they say 'pagal', *that's the first thing they'll say...'*
They all say it don't they?... My mum says it, my brother says it...
... all of them, everybody, that's the only word they got for it!

Informants stated that family members felt such people cannot be trusted with any responsibilities because they are seen as being 'without a brain', 'daft' and 'always talking rubbish'.

A few younger women, particularly those who were diagnosed as suffering from recurring bouts of post-natal depression, were sufficiently aware of their own behaviour to determine that it was not what they considered 'normal'. But even these women were deeply distressed by the possibility that the label *'pagal'* might in fact have some validity, since the drugs given to them by their GPs (family doctors) neither cured them, nor prevented recurrence of their depression.

Social effects of hospitalisation

The stigma attached to a woman who has been hospitalised can be severe in the Pakistani community, conferring what the women, their relatives and members of their community saw as a permanent negative label.[4] Bailey[5] points out that hospitalisation may be used as grounds for divorce and for looking elsewhere for a 'more fit wife and mother' (Bailey, 1993:15). One respondent stated:

our people are that type, even when a person gets better, they would still say they're 'pagal', *they would still brand them.*

Marginalisation from participation in family decisions
Since *pagal* persons are seen as being 'always out of their mind' and 'total nutters,' they tended to be excluded from family decisions. Although there is no evidence among those interviewed that women were physically ejected from the family home, there is evidence that many women are made to feel that their opinions are of little importance. Individuals feel as if their identity is negated within the family setting. Speaking of others like herself who have been in hospital one woman said:

Their existence is nil, and even in the eyes of their brothers and sisters they are nothing. He or she is not our relative.

Another woman referred to the effect her husband's long-standing diagnosed 'mental illness' has had on her own emotional health (and which resulted in her own admission to hospital):

Your own brothers and sisters say he or she is 'pagal'. He's been to 'mental' hospital and people say he's pagal, ... I get depressed, I get migraines, because I have to go to the hospital I'm labelled and people would say, 'don't listen to her she's pagal as well'.

Loss of respect

For women with younger children, family life was affected by the loss of respect on the part of children for their parent, which impaired women's ability to discipline them when necessary. According to Afshar (1994) one of the responsibilities of Muslim women towards their children is that of teacher — of history, religion, customs, and manners. Teaching children is difficult when they have lost respect for the person doing the teaching. As one woman remarked:

Sometimes when my children fight and quarrel I can't handle them. One day I told my daughter what is wrong with me, and she told her brother who then said to her, 'she's daft'. Now whenever they make a noise or fight with each other I stay quiet.

Another woman said:

My son makes mistakes, and he gets told off, but whenever my husband tells him off, he says in a low tone and in a sarcastic way, 'daft'. My son says, 'he's not in his senses, who is he to tell me what to do and what not to do?'

The woman is then open to criticism from her relatives for not being a fit mother, as another woman confirmed:

There's always something said in the family... about the children, husband or husband's parents... Therefore you think about it and make a big issue of it... Children don't respect you when they find out you're suffering from zehni bemari (mental illness).'

Stigmatisation of children

The label of *'pagal'* extends beyond individual women to affect the lives of their children. The treatment meted out to young married women, for instance, who have a parent (or parents) who have been hospitalised shows that their lives are tainted. According to one such parent:

[Even] if you get them married off...the in-laws would say they come from a pagal family, and even the children would get very parishan in their heart because people would say the whole family are pagal.

The sons-in-law not only lack respect for their in-laws (who after marriage have the same status as their parents) they insult their wives as well. She continued: 'The sons-in-law say to their wives, "you are daughter of *pagal*, you are prostitutes you are bastards".' This also causes loss of status among in-laws back in Pakistan, which is yet another source of stress and worry; as the woman concerned said, 'This is how I get very *parishan*, I keep going back to the hospital.'

Possibilities of escape

The possibility of women moving away to escape the consequences of stigmatisation is either nil or severely limited. This is not only because it is very unlikely that a woman would have financial independence, but also it may not be safe for women to leave the marital home, in the sense of leaving her husband. This would be construed as bringing dishonour on the family. At the very least such an action would cut her off from any contact with the family or at worst put her in danger from male relatives who may pursue her in an attempt to avenge the family honour.

Given that the majority of women interviewed were married, either previously or at the time of interview, such a move could only happen within the context of the whole family moving to a new area. There was no evidence from the women (or from men who were interviewed separately) that spouses wanted to move away from their present location. This may be because many people migrated to particular locations to join other family members and therefore have no wish to move elsewhere.

Social effects of medication

The discussion so far has focused on the consequences of hospitalisation, but there are other social outcomes associated with treatment with drug therapy in the community. The negative side-effects of medication have made many women unable to fulfil their domestic responsibilities such as cooking, cleaning, and shopping, or be sufficiently alert to attend to young children. Most informants described side-effects which they ascribed to their medication, which included overwhelming feelings of 'tiredness', 'sleepiness', and 'nausea'. They found it difficult to perform their household responsibilities. Cooking in particular became problematic: women were afraid to cook lest they fell asleep and exposed their toddlers to the danger of untended fires. Some women who were responsible for taking their children to and from school, as well as cooking and cleaning, found themselves unable to cope. For them, hospitalisation occurred when they were 'making a mess of things at home'.

For other women, medication had the effect of turning them into what they described as a 'dopey cow' or 'a zombie'. In addition to affecting their day-to-day functioning, this made them the subject of taunts. The humiliation of being taunted even by small children in their own communities was palpable. This very public loss of respect was distressing and demeaning not only for the women, but also their own children, who were teased by their peers for having a *'pagal'* mother.

Some older women whose young unmarried daughters lived in the same household suffered a drop in status by having to allow their daughters take over what were seen as their responsibilities. One such woman said:

... but now I can't keep up with my responsibilities. My daughter does everything. I used to do everything! I used to go in the cold weather and do all my work.

They experienced feelings of uselessness, and despair at their emotional state, which did not seem to improve with medication.

Improving organisational responses

All the women seen in this research were discharged back to their homes in the local community. The vast majority of women were referred by their GPs directly to hospital and then subsequently received, and continue to receive after-care through out-patient clinics based in psychiatric hospital. None of the women interviewed saw the relevant psychologist or psychotherapist who were also based at the hospital. After discharge therefore one had to return to the *pagal* hospital to see the doctor.

The present permanent medical staff who cater for persons whose first language is not English (as well as many other Asians who speak English fluently) are aware of the needs of the Pakistani community but face a number of constraints. Unlike other medical staff at the hospital, who have a base at mental health centres in the community, and separate staff such as social workers, community nurses, and psychologists, as well as a base in hospital, the medical staff who cater for persons for whom English is a second language operate solely from hospital. There are only a few Asian staff on the multidisciplinary team in hospital. None of the medical staff are Pakistani, although they speak patients' main 'mother-tongue' as a second language; and there is a very limited budget for interpreting for temporary medical staff working with the consultant psychiatrist.

A very small proportion of women have benefited from brief group-therapy (based in the community), but they had had to be hospitalised first, and deemed to be suffering from 'an enduring mental illness' before they could be referred to the group. They are therefore placed in a situation where in order to receive any kind of non-medical help they must first be labelled. This is a 'no-win' situation where even limited help must be preceded by hospitalisation, and the acquisition of a label, which has serious social consequences.

There is a need for a range of different services both as part of existing services, and in addition to them.[6] A handful of women in this research were benefiting from therapeutic counselling in their mother tongues, by appropriately trained personnel. Informants suggested that counselling facilities could be offered alongside the teaching of practical skills. This would make such services acceptable to spouses and other family members, and thus allow women to attend more easily. It is also crucial that such services do not label themselves as 'mental' health services, since this would defeat the very purpose of having such a facility. Counselling might also be provided in GP surgeries, through a 'primary care counsellor', so that problems could be dealt with before they reach crisis proportions, (although GPs need to be educated about how to refer appropriately).

The provision of 'Home Treatment' services in the geographical area where some of the informants live should also be considered as a valuable alternative to hospital since it allows people to be treated (including treatment and monitoring of those on medication) within their home environment. This has proved to be a beneficial method of treatment, and many studies have shown superior outcomes with home-based care compared to hospital care (Burns, 1993). It has also been shown to have great benefits in areas where there are significant proportions of people from minority ethnic groups (Muijen et al, 1992; Sashidharan and Smyth, 1992). Home-based care not only involves the family, but is shown to reduce the need for hospitalisation and the concomitant stigmatisation. All these services need to co-exist in order for clients to be referred between them according to need.

Erica Wheeler is a health researcher who has done recent work in the area of mental health. She is currently studying for a PhD. She can be contacted via The Editor, Gender and Development.

Notes

1 The methods used in the qualitative part of the research were individual interviews and women-only focus groups in the 'mother tongue' of informants.

2 Here, I can only touch on the range of various types of extended family that exist in Pakistani communities in Britain, and the details of family obligations; these are described in more detail elsewhere. Authors tend to either make reference to Pakistani communities in Britain in general (Ahmad, 1996), or concentrate on analysing kinship ties and obligations among specific Pakistani communities (Anwar, 1979; Khan, 1979). Although in some ways family roles and forms overlap with those of the white indigenous majority population, they differ substantially in many others, but have equal validity.

3 This is not mean to state definitively that all Pakistanis think this way but it has been recognised elsewhere (Afshar, 1994) that the values and indeed the beliefs of migrants tend to become ossified whereas thinking may have moved on and changed in their own countries which they left some time ago.

4 Although among a minority of women (two), there was evidence that there was some labelling prior to admission to hospital, it was clear from the stories of both those women and others interviewed, that the decisive factor in acquiring it as a permanent (and therefore a more damaging) label was the act of hospitalisation.

5 A research worker with a community based project including the same general geographical location as the one in which this study was undertaken.

6 There are two small voluntary organisations in the research locations (funded by the statutory sector) which offer counselling or support and information to Asian women. Both organisations cater for small numbers of people because their staffing and their budgets are considerably limited in comparison to the size and needs of the communities they cater for. Nationally, however, there are a growing number of voluntary organisations which cater for Asian clients

References

Afshar H. (1994) 'Muslim women in West Yorkshire' in Afshar H. and Maynard M. (eds) *The Dynamics of 'Race' and Gender*, Taylor and Francis.

Ahmad W. (1996) 'Family obligations and social change among Asian communities' in Ahmad W. and Atkin K. (eds) *'Race' and Community Care*, Open University Press, Buckingham.

Anwar M. (1979) *The Myth of Return: Pakistanis in Britain*, Heinemann, London.

Bailey S. (1993) *Women's Views of Mental Health Services*, The Cellar Project, Bradford.

Beliappa J. (1991) *Illness or Distress? Alternative Models of Mental* Health, Confederation of Indian Organisations, London.

Burns T., Beadsmore A., Bhat A. V., Oliver A. and Mathers C. (1993) 'A Controlled Ttrial of home-based acute psychiatric services I: clinical and social outcome' *British Journal of Psychiatry*, 163, pp. 49–54.

Dean C. and Gadd E.M. (1990) 'Home treatment for acute psychiatric illness' *British Medical Journal,* Vol. 301, 3 November, pp. 1021–1023.

Fenton S. and Sadiq A. (1993) *The Sorrow in My Heart*, CRE (Commission for Racial Equality), London.

Fernando S. (1991) *Mental Health, Race and Culture*, Macmillan in association with MIND, London.

Fernando S. (1992) 'Roots of racism' *Openmind 59* October/November.

Khan V. S. (1979) 'Migration and social stress: Mipuris in Bradford' in Khan. V. S (ed) *Minority Families in Britain,* Macmillan Press, London.

Muijen M., Marks I. Connolly J. and Audini B. (1992) 'Home based care and standard hospital care for patients with severe mental illness: a randomised controlled trial' *British Medical Journal* Vol. 304, 21 March.

Quddus S. A. (1995) *Family and Society in Pakistan*, Sang-E-Meel Publications, Lahore.

Rack P. (1982) *Race, Culture and Mental Disorder*, Routledge, London.

Sashidharan S. and Smyth M. (1992) *West Birmingham Home Treatment Service: Evaluation of Home Treatment in Ladywood* (Unpublished).

Sasoon M. and Lindow V. (1995) 'Consulting and empowering Black mental health system users' in Fernando S. (ed) *Mental Health in a Multi-ethnic Society*, Routledge, London.

More words but no action?

Forced migration and trafficking of women

Francine Pickup

An international conference on Trafficking of Russian and NIS Women Abroad for Prostitution was held in Moscow in November 1997. This article examines the many different perspectives that exist on the issue of trafficking, and the different policies that are linked to them, drawing on the debates at the conference to illustrate a variety of viewpoints.

The Moscow conference focused on the results of a two-year study carried out by Global Survival Network (GSN) to uncover the growing trade in Russian women for international prostitution. Prior to 1992 there were virtually no reported cases of 'trafficking'[1] of women from Russia to the West, yet, since the break-up of the Soviet Union, the phenomenon has reached 'epidemic proportions' (UN 1996, 11). While a wealth of words have been expended in the past on the problem of trafficking in the form of reports, conference recommendations,and treaties and resolutions by UN bodies, implementation of resolutions has been poor. Research and policy have been characterised by disagreement between individuals and organisations coming to the issue from very different ideological bases.

Attended by approximately 100 representatives from NGOs, governments, the United Nations, and the European Commission, the conference aimed to facilitate co-operation between Russian non-governmental groups and international NGOs, devise conference resolutions for govern-

ments and non-state actors, and undertake activities to address the problem of trafficking.

The research for the conference drew on interviews with NGOs and over 50 women who had been trafficked overseas, and police and government officials in Russia, Europe, Asia, and the US. These were combined with less conventional methodologies, used to discover how the traffickers operated, such as setting up a dummy company that specialised in importing foreign women as entertainers and escorts, and the filming of dealings with traffickers using hidden cameras.

This article argues that the violence and abuses linked to sex work are due to stigmatisation of prostitution, and the unequal power relations involved in the work, at all levels: from the point of view of the women themselves, and between sending and receiving countries and regions. Appropriate policy responses should therefore be based on an empowering approach; increasing women's opportunities to help themselves is a more effective use of resources to prevent trafficking than the abolitionist strategies of the past.

Perspectives on a contested concept

The trafficking phenomenon has been perceived differently by individuals, organisations, and political groupings: in relation to organised crime, illegal migration, prostitution, forced labour, violence against women, unequal economic relationships, and poverty.

In the last century, the concept of 'traffic in women' was linked to 'white slavery'. The 1904 International Agreement for the Suppression of the White Slave aimed to combat the procuring of women and girls for immoral purposes abroad by compulsion.[2] In 1949, the United Nations Convention for the Suppression of the Traffic in Persons and of the Exploitation of the Prostitution of Others stated, 'prostitution (is) incompatible with the dignity and worth of the human person'. It obliged states parties to punish any person who 'to gratify the passions of another, (p)rocures, entices or leads away, for purposes of prostitution, another person, even with the consent of that person'.

The Convention reflected the abolitionist sentiment still prevailing in the first half of the twentieth century, understanding the woman solely as victim: if abuses are inherent in migrant prostitution, then governments must abolish both prostitution and trafficking. However, the assumption behind the Convention — that if you get rid of the demand, by prosecuting third parties involved, supply will wither away — is simplistic. It ignores the problem of the need to earn a living — 'structural coercion'.[3] Women may choose to migrate for work, and to enter prostitution because of poverty and lack of alternative employment opportunities.

In Russia this has particular resonance, as women experience disproportionately high rates of unemployment. In 1991, unemployment was estimated at 40 per cent (Standing, 1994) with 71 of the unemployed being women (Fong and Paull 1992).

Such high rates of female unemployment explain the comment made by Elena Tiuriukanova (from the Institute of Socio-Economic Studies of Population, Moscow) at the conference: that migrant prostitution is a livelihood strategy employed by some women, 'not just a way to get money but a strategy for life'.

Feminist perspectives on trafficking

In the 1980s, trafficking became a focus of attention again because of concern over the spread of AIDS, and feminist research on sexual exploitation. In feminist circles, trafficking is a highly contentious issue. The conflict over language — 'sex work' or 'prostitution', and 'migration' or 'trafficking' goes to the heart of the debate over whether prostitution is a valid job option, or a form of violence against women. The debate hinges on the distinction between sex-related work and other forms of labour.

The Dutch Foundation Against Trafficking in Women (STV), aims to protect the human rights of sex workers and recognise sex work as a legitimate form of work: 'it would be useful to consider [seeing]..."commercial sex workers" [as] labour issues and not an issue of violence against women' (STV, 1996, 1). The policy implications of this approach can be legalisation and regulatory legislation, as in the Netherlands, where brothels have recently been decriminalised.[4] STV distinguishes between forced and free prostitution, and between prostitution and trafficking. The Beijing Platform For Action that emerged from the 1995 Fourth World Women's Conference makes a similar distinction, condemning violence against women, yet exempting prostitution *per se* from the category of human rights violations, instead condemning only 'forced prostitution'. The Platform also distinguishes between trafficking and prostitution, calling for sanctions only against trafficking.

A second feminist constituency takes the abolitionist position, arguing that all forms of trafficking and prostitution are inherently forced and constitute violence against women. Organisations such as the Campaign Against Trafficking in Women (CATW) argue that governments and funders only perpetuate exploitation if they adhere to the distinction between forced and free prostitution, as this allows the legitimising and increased commercialisation of prostitution,[5] and encourages the growth in trafficking. However, the abolitionist approach has been criticised as 'a fundamental misconception about what constitutes slavery and what prostitution' (Bindman 1997, p.4). Bindman argues that the international definition of slavery is based on an enduring employer-employee relationship and the employer's abuse of superior power. The commercial transaction between the sex worker and client is, however, not characterised by employment relations; the client is a customer, and the relationship is limited in time and scope.

Towards clearer definitions

In 1996, in a report requested by the UN Special Rapporteur on Violence Against Women, the Global Alliance Against Trafficking in Women (GAATW) developed definitions of trafficking and forced labour or slavery in line with the liberal approach of the first of the two sides in the feminist debate. This definition emphasises coercion, and explicitly distinguishes trafficking from forced labour and slavery-like practices. Trafficking is defined as, 'all acts involved in the recruitment and/or transportation of a woman within and across national borders for work or services by means of violence or the threat of violence, abuse of authority or dominant position, debt bondage, deception and other forms of coercion' (Wijers & Lap-Chew, 1997 p.36).

The definition of forced labour and slavery-like practices covers forced prostitution: 'the extraction of work and services from any woman or the appropriation of the legal identity and/or physical person of any woman by means of violence or the threat of violence, abuse of

authority or dominant position, debt bondage, deception or other forms of coercion' (Wijers & Lap-Chew, 1997 p.36).

These definitions take coercion[6] as the critical element: they see the problem as the exploitative and abusive power relations which may be associated with the international journey to sell sex and the act of selling it, rather than the journey or the work in themselves.

Deconstructing organisational agendas

This section examines the various perspectives on trafficking represented at the Moscow conference, with a view to understanding the impact of the associated potential policies for the women concerned.

State responses to trafficking

Trafficking as organised crime

Russia is a receiving and transit country, as well as a sending country. Women are trafficked to Russia from the Ukraine, Belorussia, and Kazakhstan. The Russian *propiska* system, whereby a person cannot be employed in a region without a residence permit, increases women's vulnerability to trafficking. Unemployed women from the provinces come to Moscow but cannot obtain a residence permit because they do not have the money or family connections in the urban area that are necessary. Often women without permits enter prostitution, and either go under the control of police, or seek protection from criminal gangs. One recommendation to come from the conference is a review of the *propiska* system, and legislation on internal movement.

The UN Centre for International Crime Prevention views trafficking as an example of organised crime. In Russia, as well as recruiting, transporting and distributing the women, Russian criminal groups provide protection for trafficking operations and sex businesses. On deciding to travel abroad for work, a woman is likely to turn to one of the many employment agencies, entertainment companies, or marriage agencies which specialise in placing women with foreign employers. These are often illegal companies, run by organised criminal groups, which manipulate and mislead the women. At the conference, Michael Platzer, Chief, Operational Activities at the Centre, stated that 'prostitution and trafficking in women is still the biggest money-maker for organised crime groups in Eastern Europe'. Tackling trafficking by bringing criminals to justice has proved a very difficult and expensive task, and has yielded little success. This approach is also based on the assumption that in tackling demand, the supply of women will disappear; and therefore ignores the fact that women enter the trafficking process in order to find work and earn an income.

Conference participants pointed out that this strategy reflects the current popularity of the criminal law as an instrument to solve social problems. A criminal approach is appealing to states, as they are then seen to be tackling the problem. As a result, the state is released from taking more difficult preventative and remedial measures, that effectively meet the women's interests.

Trafficking as illegal migration

The international nature of trafficking means the power of an individual state to combat the problem is limited. One way is to use laws on migration. However, migration legislation is heavily influenced by prevailing economic and political interests. This approach depicts trafficked women as criminals who have crossed borders illegally or are illegal residents; policies in response will protect the interests of the state, and not those of the women.

Xenophobic actions by receiving countries to combat trafficking in women, such as tightening visa policies, limiting residence and labour permits, and bringing in more instruments for the detention and expulsion of persons without residence permits, make it harder for women to obtain visas legally, and therefore play into the hands of traffickers. A further problem with framing trafficking as a problem of illegal border crossing is that women often enter countries legally as tourists, brides or entertainers.

There are various articles in the Russian criminal code that could be used to assist women who have been trafficked. Lyudmila Zavadskaya, the Deputy Minister of Justice, explained that the Ministry had made 80 bilateral agreements with other countries to combat this 'latent criminality'. These agreements state that a person from another country should enjoy the same rights as a citizen of the host country. However, Olga Samarina, the Head of the Ministry of Labour, explained, 'Women will not apply for legal aid as outlined in the bilateral agreements mentioned by the Deputy Minister of Justice, because it is likely that they will be deported. If women do apply for legal aid at the consulate, they often have to wait months for it to materialise. In the meantime they continue to be exploited and could be resold.' The conference recommended strengthening such bilateral agreements by making them public and so more available to NGOs working with trafficked women.

Human rights campaigners at the conference argued that corruption or inaction on the part of government can legitimise trafficking. Participants cited cases of police being bribed not to arrest pimps; forgery of visas of women to be trafficked; state officials paid protection money; and arbitrary detention. Participants also described cases amounting to torture, for example, the rape in custody of trafficked women who were working as prostitutes.

Participants called for governments in receiving countries to be responsible for providing information and legal assistance to the trafficked women, rather than detaining or deporting them. Governments should focus on strengthening good

48

practices, such as supporting women's human rights, rather than enforcing repressive strategies such as restrictive immigration policies.

Using international law

A wide range of international laws and standards apply to trafficking in women and children for prostitution, domestic work, bonded labour, and servile forms of marriage (Wijers & Lap-Chew, 1997). The 1993 Declaration on the Elimination of All Forms of Violence Against Women states that 'trafficking in women and forced labour are violations of women's human rights, for which states are accountable in the public and private spheres; governments should be held accountable for perpetuating or condoning trafficking in women'. However, in its present form, the 1993 Declaration is of limited use, as it has not been ratified, and cannot be used to hold states accountable for their actions.

NGO responses to trafficking

How do NGOs respond to the needs of women involved in international sex-work? A crucial question, especially for funding agencies, is whether they should support prostitutes' groups and organisations geared to support trafficked and migrant women through educational campaigns, legal advice centres, and so implicitly support sex-work as a valid job option. In practice, the opposite course of action is more usual: international organisations concerned with fighting poverty and injustice, such as Oxfam, have responded by supporting projects to provide health care and training for alternative livelihoods (Oxfam internal documents 1997). However, this is to implicitly adopt the abolitionist position, that all sex work is inherently abusive, regardless of the circumstances.

Another strategy is to support educational work and consciousness-raising on trafficking and forced prostitution. The conference heard from grassroots NGOs in Eastern Europe who have focused on awareness-raising about the dangers of seeking jobs abroad, in schools with potentially vulnerable girls. For example, La Strada is a Kiev-based[7] organisation that is trying to stem the growing traffic of Ukrainian women to work in foreign sex industries. It informs potential migrants of their human rights, produces public information leaflets and posters about trafficking, operates a telephone hotline, and provides counselling. Olga Shved from La Strada, Ukraine, speaking at the conference, explained 'the problem that we face is that we cannot guarantee safety to the women coming to us. We cannot provide anonymous shelter. The other problem for women who want to return is that parents tell their daughters not to come back, for fear that they will put the whole family in danger.'

The conference participants reached a consensus that there needed to be more prevention and education campaigns that target groups of women and girls in schools at risk of recruitment in areas where there is high unemployment. There also needs to be more support programmes for women returning after trafficking, that provide counselling, hotlines for crisis intervention, legal advice, and shelter for those in danger of reprisals from criminal groups.

An anthropological approach to sex and violence

The concept of trafficking implies that the women involved are passive victims. However, it appears that there is an element of choice for women in determining their livelihoods, and that sex-work can be a rational economic option. But how can we understand women's choice to migrate for sex-work when it is not primarily out of poverty and a lack of alternatives? The conference noted that, at the very least, the range of sex-related work (telephone sex, beauty contests, modelling, hotel prostitution, video pornography) currently carried out by Russian women suggests that a broader definition of sex-work is required than 'provision of sexual services for payment' is required.

In a 1993 survey of Moscow's female school-leavers, it was reported that in answer to the question 'which is the most attractive profession?', 60 per cent replied 'prostitution' (Argumenty i fakty 1993, 7). Is the way sex work is currently being seen in Eastern Europe different to its stigmatised image in Western countries?

Here, anthropological approaches may help us to understand the way women's life choices are determined by their specific context, including the particular significance attached to women's bodies. The so-called 'resexualisation' of society (Corrin, 1992) is often portrayed as liberating for women, because it allows them to discover their suppressed sexuality. For Russian women, this is epitomised by the fact that they can now buy lipstick in the shops, like their Western counterparts.

Neo-liberal economists endorse the growth of the sex industry as an embodiment of the reform process and the new social freedoms that accompany this, challenging the constraints imposed by the state in the past. The increasing number of women entering the sex industry has been seen as a sign of progress, demonstrating that women are practising entrepreneurial virtues of new liberalism (Kiss, 1992). In contrast, some Russian commentators have treated women who engage in this kind of behaviour as symbols of the times: epitomising material vulnerability, moral confusion, the cultural imperialism of the West, and the degradation of the Russian nation.

In selling sex, therefore, the Russian woman sex-worker embodies an apparent contradiction between newly-liberated feminine sexuality, aggressive market orientation, and confused moral identity. How women see themselves in relation to

these conflicting understandings, and how they are identified by others, has important resource and policy implications for the state and non-governmental welfare and social institutions.

Conclusion

The Moscow conference illustrates the importance of disentangling the various agendas that have influenced the definition of trafficking, in order to pin-point whose interests are being served by the corresponding policies. It is also important to understand all aspects of the trafficking process, in order to identify which practices should be combated, with a view to protecting women from specific instances of violence. At the same time, it is also important to view trafficking in women holistically, as a cycle that begins before women leave their country of origin, encompasses their experiences in the host country, and continues after their return.

The conference provided a valuable opportunity for exchange and coalition-building between the new, independent Russian women's organisations, through discussion of a problem that has not until now been widely recognised in Russia.[8] But the focus must move from words expended at ministerial meetings and international conferences, to the creation of the opportunities for action by different constituencies, including women's organisations. It must be recognised that women's motives for entering the trafficking cycle, and their self-help responses to break out of that cycle, are two sides of the same coin. Initiatives which approach the problem of trafficking as an organised crime or a migration issue ignore the most important opportunities to support women who are trafficked. Policy should build on women's coping mechanisms as a part of the solution to combating the violence, exploitation, and abuse of women in the trafficking process. Empowering policy should target preventative education initiatives and support the trafficked women on their return home.

Notes

1 The term 'trafficking' is used critically in this article, acknowledging that it is linked to a conception of the state as concerned with matters of security and national boundaries. In addition, the concept of 'trafficked woman' is problematic as it tends to render the woman passive. These issues will be addressed further in this article.

2 The condition of constraint, implied by the use of the term 'compulsive', was removed in the 1993 International Convention for the Suppression in Traffic in Women, but this only applies to the international traffic in women.

3 My thanks to Ashwani Saith who suggested this concept to explain women's initiative in a situation that poses considerable constraints.

4 The problem with this approach had been that it leads to a two-tier system whereby Dutch prostitutes are protected by the state and Third World women are trafficked into the country illegally. The state lowers the market value of legal European prostitutes to promote local prostitutes and thus is driving a rift between women from Europe and those from the Third World.

5 See for example, Raymond, J. 'Prostitution as Violence Against Women' in *Women's Global Network for Reproductive Rights*, Newsletter 60 1997 #4. It is certainly true that some governments, especially in South East Asia, are guilty of institutionalising prostitution and sex-tourism, through their tacit approval of market structures and networks which promote it, to increase business and the remission of foreign currency.

6 Coercion can take various forms including, but not limited to, violence or the threat of violence, including the deprivation of freedom of movement and personal choice; deception, such as the nature of the work to be done; abuse of authority, such as confiscating personal documents; and debt bondage.

7 At the conference, Olga Shved from La Strada stated that in Kiev in 1995, the police had 400 cases of parents looking for their daughters, who were thought to have gone abroad.

8 For more information on the response of local crisis centres and women's organisations in Russia to issues such as domestic violence and rape, please refer to Khodyreva, N. (1996) 'Sexism and Sexual Abuse in Russia', in Corrin, C. (ed.) *Women in a Violent World: Feminist Analyses and Resistance Across 'Europe'* and Zabelina, T. (1996) 'Sexual Violence Towards Women', in Pilkington, H. (ed.) *Gender, Generation and Identity in Contemporary Russia* .

References

Bindman, J (1993) *Forced Prostitution in Turkey: Women in the Genelevs*, ASI Human Rights Series No. 6, Anti-Slavery International, London UK.

'Besplatnykh zavtrakov ne byvaet' 1993, Argumenty i fakty 1:7

CATW (Coalition Against Trafficking In Women) 1991, 16th Session of the Working Group on Contemporary Forms of Slavery in 1991, UN Economic and Social Council E/CN.4/Sub2/1991/41.

Corrin, C (1992) *Superwoman and the Double Burden: Women's Experience of Change in Central and Eastern Europe and the Former Soviet Union* London, Scarlet Press

Fong, M and Paull, G (1992) *The Changing Role of Women in Employment in Eastern Europe*, World Bank, Europe and Central Asia Region, Population and Human Resources Division, Report No. 8213, February

Kiss, Y (1992) 'The second "No": women in Hungary', *Feminist Review* note 13, pp 49–57

Standing, G (1994) *Labour Markets Dynamics in Russian Industry in 1993: Results from the Third Round of the RLFS*, Budapest, ILO-CEET

STV, Foundation Against Trafficking in Women (1995) *New Bulletin* 2:1–8.

STV International *News Bulletin* 1 March 1996, 1

Wijers, M and Lap-Chew, L (1997) *Trafficking in Women, Forced Labour and Slavery-like Practices in Marriage, Domestic Labour and Prostitution*, Report following initial international investigation carried out by STV and GAATW and presented to United Nations Special Rapporteur on Violence Against Women, Mrs. Radhika Coomerswamy, in November 1996.

The use and abuse of female domestic workers from Sri Lanka in Lebanon

Lina Abu-Habib

In Lebanon today, large numbers of Sri Lankan women are employed as domestic servants, many of whom suffer abuse and violence. This article asks why NGOs in Lebanon do not seem to be concerned about this situation, and suggests what might be done to address the needs of migrants.

'You know, I do not really care for tea, but my friend Mala does. Her employers forbid her to drink tea or any other drink all day long. They would only allow her to eat leftovers. When they used to go out and leave her alone at home, they used to lock the door and fridge and tie her hands. I do not understand — why tie her hands when the main door and everything else in the house are locked?'
Siani, a 36-year-old Sri Lankan domestic worker in Lebanon

In Lebanon today, being a woman domestic worker from Sri Lanka means facing gender, class, and race discrimination simultaneously. Given the lack of legal rights or social support for these workers, the situation is reminiscent of slavery. Sadly, however, it does not seem to be important enough to stir the interest of organisations working on other humanitarian or human rights issues.

Some years ago, I heard a woman representative of a 'progressive' political party give a public address. While complaining about the treatment of other people living in Lebanon without citizenship, she said '...and I want the world to know that we the [.....] are treated in Lebanon as if we were Sri Lankans!' This statement may have gone unnoticed had it not been for a listener who was equally seen as progressive, who was quick to retort '...may God forbid, never have we treated you as Sri Lankans!'

This article examines the lack of support given by humanitarian and human rights organisations in Lebanon to women domestic workers from Sri Lanka. Despite their increased visibility, the predicament and tragedy of this relatively large and predominantly female community remains virtually ignored. This article describes the different forms of gender, ethnic, and class discrimination to which many female domestic workers are constantly subjected, and asks why their increased vulnerability does not appear to be a cause for concern on the part of local or international NGOs. The article ends by suggesting approaches which NGOs could take to address the plight of women migrant workers.

The road from Sri Lanka to Beirut

It was only after the onset of the Gulf War in 1990, which led to the repatriation of tens of thousands of migrant workers, that the West became aware of the tragedy of Asian domestic workers in Kuwait and other host countries in the region. Tales of slavery, forced prostitution, and inhumane treatment made media headlines for a short time. Now, a few years later, the public consciousness around the world has been stirred by individual cases, such as the execution of a Filipina domestic worker in Singapore and the public flogging of another Filipina in the UAE who had killed her employer in self-defence as he was trying to rape her, reminding the world of the thousands of women stranded away from home with no legal or social support. These horror stories, however, are not limited to one particular host country or to Southern women in Northern countries. This article draws on my own experience, and observation of and direct contact with, Sri Lankan women workers in Lebanon. According to Ministry of Labour statistics, Sri Lankan migrants, of whom the majority are women domestic workers, constitute more than half the legal migrant force in Lebanon. This is confirmed by newspaper reports that, of a total of 47,974 work-permits granted to foreigners in the first 10 months of 1997, 19,602 were for Sri Lankan domestic workers, mostly women (*Al Dyar*, 25 December 1997).

It is difficult to trace the history of the influx into Lebanon of migrant workers from Sri Lanka or any other Asian or African country as there is very little documentation or research, which in itself testifies to the lack of awareness and minimal importance of imported labour. However, based on empirical evidence and personal accounts, the major influx started in the late 1970s (Brochmann 1993), when the civil war in Lebanon was accompanied by a gradual paralysis in state function and control. The deterioration of the economy and a crisis in security encouraged Arab domestic workers (mostly from Syria and Egypt) to leave Lebanon, thus creating a gap which was rapidly filled by cheaper Asian migrant labour, particularly from Sri Lanka. Sri Lankan women, and to a much lesser extent Sri Lankan men, were the first to come *en masse* through illegal or semi-legal channels, typically involving employment agencies in Lebanon and Sri Lanka, brokers, and middlemen, including government officials (Achkar-Noccocho 1997). This migration was tacitly encouraged by the government of Sri Lanka; as for most 'sending' countries, migrant labour plays a significant role in the economy, including offsetting the external debt-service payment, because of foreign exchange remittances (Rodrigo and Jayatissa 1989). In fact, migration simultaneously produces 'dependence for both the sending state and for the individual involved' (Brochman, 1993, 172).

Many people's food, education, health care, and even lives back home depend on the hard work of these migrant women (Chant 1992). This is borne out from my own discussions with women domestic workers. An overwhelming majority are married, and have left their children in the care of their immediate families, in-laws, or other relatives. A wide circle of relatives often depends on the remittances of the domestic workers.

Catalogue shopping for maids

For a family in Lebanon, the procurement process is relatively simple and efficient. A first contact is made with a local employment agency, which offers a selection of pictures of Sri Lankan girls for prospective employers to choose from. The employer then pays a lump sum of up to GBP 2000 to the agency to cover their fees, the airfare, and a 'deposit'. Once the payment is settled, the employment agency arranges for the Sri Lankan woman to be brought to Lebanon, helps to secure a passport in Sri Lanka, and facilitates entrance to Lebanon (personal communication, 1998).

Cumaranatunga has identified three stages at which problems and pressures are experienced by women from Sri Lanka seeking employment as domestic workers abroad (Cumaranatunga 1990). The first of these is before their departure from Sri Lanka, when women often become involved in an illegal process of paying bribes to employment agencies and to unscrupulous government officials, borrowing money from loansharks, and falsifying passports and travel documents. Some women are particularly likely to need to falsify documents — including minors, and those wanting to change their religious affiliation to make them more 'acceptable' to certain employers (internal Oxfam report, 1997).

Problems in Lebanon

The second set of problems are faced on arrival in the host country. One can imagine the confusion and panic of women, many of whom had never left their villages before, arriving in a foreign country, where nobody speaks their language, and where they have no social support system. Upon her arrival in Lebanon, the Sri Lankan maid is handed over to her new employers, who are responsible for securing the necessary residency and work permit (Achkar-Noccocho, 1997). During the first few months of employment, if the employers do not 'like' their new maid for any reason, or if she happens to have any health or other problem, she may be 'returned' to the employment agency, who will ensure that she is quickly 'replaced'. There is no official information about what happens to women who are 'returned' to employment agencies; but clearly, neither the agency nor the employer are willing to lose on the investment paid for bringing a maid all the way from Sri Lanka; hence, every effort is made to ensure that the woman is re-employed in any way possible (personal communications with activists working on the issue, 1998).

Sri Lankan domestic workers who come on contracts typically lasting three years are paid up to $100 per month. They do not have access to any employment benefits nor are they protected by local labour laws. There have been numerous reported cases of employers witholding payment either temporarily or even indefinitely (ibid). Sri Lankan migrant workers to Lebanon find themselves in an alien environment, where not only practical aspects of life such as food are unfamiliar, but they are often not permitted to fulfil their religious devotions, regardless of whether they are Christian or Muslim (personal communication with domestic workers, 1997). The distress caused is relatively mild in comparison to the suffering of those who encounter physical and psychological abuse. Testimonies from many domestic workers speak of cruel and inhumane treatment, as well as long working hours, intimidation, and confiscation of passports and travel documents (ibid).

In the case of abuse, there is very little that a Sri Lankan maid can do except run away without her passport and travel documents. She may be picked up by the all-too-numerous prostitution rings; if she is luckier, she may become self-employed, hiring her services as a daily maid to employers of her own choice. Although this arrangement is slightly more lucrative, it is risky, as women without travel documents can be apprehended by the security forces at any time, and are likely to be deported.

Once back home, domestic workers face a third set of difficulties. According to an assessment undertaken by the Oxfam Office in Colombo with a number of local NGOs working with returnees (Oxfam, 1997), many women are stigmatised on return to their own communities, as they are assumed to have led a promiscuous life abroad. According to workers who have stayed in touch with friends who have returned home, returnees commonly complain about husbands taking on mistresses during their absence, or about tension and conflicts with an unemployed spouse. In short, Sri Lankan migrant workers to the Middle East make 'few long-term gains in terms of status, autonomy, fewer burdens or enduring economic security' (Brochmann 1993, 178).

Presenting alternatives to labour migration

The prevention of the appalling treatment of migrant domestic workers has been very much a concern of women's groups in other sending countries, including the Philippines, who have pressured their government to take action to prohibit migration, particularly to the Middle East. Unfortunately, the government of Sri Lanka has yet to take similar action regarding migration to Lebanon; there has been some discussion of this, but no definite plans (personal communications with activists, November/December 1997). This issue is of increasing concern especially after the famous case of the Sri Lankan honorary consul in Jordan, a Jordanian citizen, who was tried, but found innocent, on more than 80 charges of trafficking in Sri Lankan women and children.

Whilst the governments of both sending and host countries need to take serious and immediate action to protect women migrant workers, local and international NGOs and women's groups and networks need to take a stronger position on this issue. There is an immediate need for organisations working with a women's rights focus to undertake field research on the situation of women migrant workers in Lebanon, and upon their return to Sri Lanka. If women are going back to Sri Lanka with very little gained in economic terms, then the myth of the 'eldorado' should be challenged, through grassroots awareness-raising. NGOs need to publicise the situation of Sri Lankan migrant women in order to discourage the exodus. More also needs to be done in the international arena, to denounce this situation and put pressure on governments to sign and ratify international conventions for the protection of migrant workers.

NGOs' responses

Until recently, no local NGO in Lebanon has actively engaged in any form of work with women migrant workers from Sri Lanka or any other sending country. Since early 1997, the newly-established Lebanese League to Resist Violence Against Women has been running a telephone 'hot-line' for women victims of violence; it is also involved with media campaigning on violence, and advocacy on law reforms, and is increasingly publicising the needs of women who are particularly vulnerable to violence: notably women with disabilities, migrant women, and women refugees.

Laksetha (in Sinhali 'Well-being') is the only centre for Sri Lankan and other migrant workers, mostly women, in Lebanon. It is run by a dedicated and undefeatable nun from Sri Lanka of the Good Shepherd Congregation. The centre is the last resort for Sri Lankan women in despair. Many are runaways and hence their legal status has to be resolved, which is no easy matter especially if their passports and travel documents have been confiscated by employers. Many others are seriously ill and need to be repatriated immediately. Many are having to return home after years of strenuous work, with no money and often no possessions except the clothes they are wearing. Tina Naccache, one of the very few human rights activists working with Sri Lankan migrant women in Laksetha, says that 'although some

56

measures of control are being introduced and which is indeed a positive sign, yet the lives of Sri Lankan women are not getting any better. The number of complaints is not decreasing and what is worrying is that we are seeing signs of new developing problems such as increased prostitution and pregnancies'. In addition, Naccache reports being asked for 'Sri Lankan' babies for adoption, a matter which is highly unlikely. Naccache fears that the increase in illegitimate, unrecognised, and unregistered half-Sri-Lankan children will undoubtedly attract worldwide trafficking in children.

Apart from these two examples, organisational responses to the interests and needs of migrant domestic workers are largely lacking. In the course of my work with Oxfam GB in Lebanon, and my discussions with different NGOs and women groups involved in rights issues, I have often been amazed by the reaction when I suggest that the abuses faced by women domestic workers are serious and that we should address them in the NGO community. Comments reveal the confused emotions and thoughts surrounding the topics of labour migration and domestic work, and the way in which these women face class, race and gender discrimination simultaneously, and reactions vary between denial, rejection, or lack of interest.

Typical statements include: 'they came here of their own free will', 'they would have starved to death in their countries',

'they're stealing jobs away from Lebanese', 'they complain too much and are ungrateful, they deserve it all', and 'they are thieves and liars, and I cannot believe that they are beaten and raped by their employers'. It is unusual to have such views expressed without apology by development workers and activists; many of whom are women.

References

Achjar-Noccocho, T (1997) 'Who does the dishes and at what cost? Paid and unpaid domestic work in Lebanon', unpublished paper presented at the Gender and Citizenship Conference, Beirut, March 1997.

Brochmann G (1993) *Middle East Avenue: Female Migration from Sri Lanka to the Gulf*, Westview Press

Chant S, (1992) *Gender and Migration in Developing Countries*, Belhaven Press.

Cumaranatunga L K (1990) 'Coping with the unknown: Sri Lankan domestic aides' in Kiribamune S and Samarasinghe V, *Women at the Crossroads: a Sri Lankan Perspective* International Centre for Ethnic Studies, Colombo.

Rodrigo C and Jayatissa R A, (1989) 'Maximising benefits from Labour Migration: Sri Lanka', in Amjad R (ed), *To the Gulf and Back: Studies on the Economic Impact of Asian Labour Migration*, ILO/ARTEP.

Migration, ethnicity and conflict:

Oxfam's experience of working with Roma communities in Tuzla, Bosnia-Hercegovina

Alex Jones[1]

The article draws on the experience of Oxfam GB in Tuzla, Bosnia-Hercegovina in researching and working with Roma communities, and focuses on the changes in the role of women as a result of the recent conflict.

Around the world, Roma people (often referred to as Romanies or Gypsies) are popularly seen as nomadic, with constant migration as their way of life (Crowe 1996). For Roma people in former Yugoslavia, this simplistic assumption not only ignores the reality of life for many, who do not lead nomadic ways of life, but underplays the shock to the community caused by forced migration and settlement as a result of the conflict.

The context

Roma people as a group are living in a very difficult situation and are, to a large extent, socially marginalised. Lack of knowledge about the nature and causes of this marginalisation could be seen in two consecutive strategic planning sessions in Oxfam, in 1995 and 1996. Roma people were identified by Oxfam staff as marginalised, but the reasons for marginalisation remained unclear: 'One Roma community which lived in the middle of Tuzla were not accessing relief distributions; we needed to take a closer look to see why' (information from Usha Kar, former Oxfam GB Bosnia Country Representative, 1998).

In May 1996, Oxfam GB (formerly Oxfam UK/I) commissioned a researcher, Dinka Masic, who had previously worked with Roma people in Macedonia, to work with local Roma people to collect information about their situation and needs. The primary aim of Oxfam's research was to investigate how accessible Oxfam's projects had been thus far to Roma people, and to identify what other forms of assistance were needed. The research was also seen as an opportunity to collect information for advocacy work, and to raise awareness of the situation of Roma people.

At the time of the research, no organised groups among Roma people could be identified to work with. The researcher contacted Roma communities in the Tuzla area to begin the process of collecting information. The research involved about 1,000 Roma women, men and children in Tuzla, who were encouraged to define their situation and needs themselves. Much time has been spent with the communities — particularly with women — discussing what kind of support is useful and effective.

Although humanitarian aid (in the form of relief distributions) was clearly expressed as a need, the Roma people also sought support to access their rights and to challenge prejudice and discrimination, as these, for them, were the underlying causes of their poverty and powerlessness. Many Roma people are hesitant to be open about their background and culture, for fear of further prejudice. There are therefore some limitations to the scope and depth of this article, from the very nature of social relationships between the Roma community and the wider world.

Life before the conflict

Historically, Roma people — also known as 'gypsies' have been relegated to low social and economic status in the countries of Eastern Europe (Crowe 1996). Roma people identify themselves as ethnically Roma yet can be Orthodox or Catholic Christians, or Muslims. Despite the significant influence of their culture on Eastern European music and art, they have not commanded respect from other ethnic groups. Prejudice has taken the form of social and economic marginalisation and also of organised violence, notably the genocide known as the Porajmos ('Gypsy holocaust') between 1933 and 1945, when an estimated 26,000 – 28,000 people died in the territory which in 1941 became the Independent State of Croatia (NDH)[2]. Of the 60,000 Roma who lived in Serbia before World War Two, 12,000 died in the Porajmos (ibid.).

In former Yugoslavia, only Bosnia and Montenegro came to recognise Roma as a distinct national group in their constitutions; the constitutions of Yugoslavia's other four republics continued to identify them only as an ethnic group. The status of 'nationality' enabled Roma people to establish schools where teaching was in their own mother tongue, to defend themselves in court in their mother tongue, and to media produce in their own language. However, in Bosnia, recognition of Roma as a distinct ethnic

group was arguably used more as a tool for their segregation within society than in order to recognise them as equal citizens of a society which respected their culture and way of life. The gradual political, economic and social breakdown of the Yugoslav state in the 1980s, and existing prejudice towards Roma people, served to increase hostility and violence towards them (ibid.).

Economically, Roma people are among the most marginalised groups in society, with the highest unemployment rate of any community in Tuzla (interview with staff, Centre For Social Work, Tuzla, 1996). While Roma people are often popularly believed to lead a nomadic existence, the reality is more complex. Some Roma stayed in one place, usually those with a specific trade or craft, whereas the nomadic Roma travelled to wherever there was a fair or festival, to tell fortunes and to trade in gifts. However, the romantic image of gypsy nomads, as given in traditional folk-tales, is misleading; Roma society is not static but dynamic, reacting to change. Roma people have taken note of changing economic circumstances, identifying new services including car-washing, and new markets. Many Roma have switched their attendance at overcrowded rural town markets to the bigger market in Sarajevo (Masic 1996).

The impact of conflict on Roma life

Mobility and settlement

Since the war, there are no reliable data kept on the number of Roma people in Bosnia-Hercegovina, as no official census has been carried out. Two years after the signing of the Dayton Peace Agreement and the end of hostilities, despite efforts by Oxfam, it has been impossible to get any accurate information from the local authorities about the number of Roma people living in any one area. This has undoubtedly been complicated by the Roma people's reluctance to give information for fear of prejudice and persecution. In an attempt to resolve this, Oxfam has helped Roma groups to establish databases of Roma people and to carry out a census in the Tuzla area (Federation of BiH) and Bijeljina (Republika Srpska of BiH).

Informants in the research confirmed that traditional migratory movement was brought to a halt with the outbreak of war. For some, migration to a third country (primarily Germany), and continuing movement within it, was their chosen option; it is unclear how many people left. Problems face those who now wish to return, who may find other displaced people have taken over their houses. In the case of Bjeljina, a small town in north-east Bosnia, the majority of the large pre-war Roma community left during the war to go to Germany. Many of their houses are now occupied by displaced Serbs from the Muslim-Croat Federation, one of the two new entities created from Bosnia-Herzegovina on the signing of the Dayton Peace Agreement in 1995, the other being Republika Srpska.

The new constitution, drawn up as a result of the Dayton Peace Agreement, has removed the three-tier ranking mentioned above, effectively removing the recognised national status Roma people had in society. For Roma people, this has meant they are forced to migrate to the part of Bosnia associated with their ethnic background; no consideration was made for people who did not categorise themselves as Serb, Muslim or Croat. Zone of separation areas (ZOS) between the two entities are heavily mined, preventing border crossings. For all displaced people in Bosnia, the 750,000 landmines on the territory of Bosnia-Hercegovina have removed the chance for any temporary settlements on abandoned land.

Economic change

The post-war ethnic pattern of regionalisation and the halt to population movement means an end to the pattern of economic migration that took place before the war. In later research in 1997, almost half the respondents stated that when income was insufficient for a family, their families would

have moved to another area to seek employment; this figure is now just 6 per cent (Oxfam research, November/December 1997). Fairs and festivals have yet to resume; these were not only traditionally significant for livelihoods but for social interaction (meeting friends and relatives) and cultural events such as marriages.

Changes to gender relations and women's role

Of all the changes that the war has brought to the lives of the Roma people, the impact to the social status and economic role of women has perhaps been the most dramatic. Current data show the employment rate of the Roma population in Tuzla at 3 per cent (of which 2.8 per cent are men) (Oxfam research, 1996). However, despite this ostensibly low employment rate as compared to men, the war has brought about an emphasis on women as the main providers; many men fled the country or fought and were killed during the war. In the research, women and men both thought the effects of this unemployment have largely fallen on women; Roma men now lean on women to provide for the whole family, while maintaining their traditional role in the home.

In most Roma communities, there remains a very clear distinction between concepts of 'men's work' and 'women's work'. In the immediate pre-war period, Roma women looked after their own households and took care of children, begging, and sometimes providing domestic help to other households outside of the Roma community, at an extremely low wage, and with no regulations regarding working conditions, despite labour laws designed to prevent this (Masic, 1996).

Large numbers of internally displaced people and a post-war economic crisis have resulted in a drop in the number of Roma women employed. At the same time a dramatic drop in the standard of living and the average income in Bosnia has also seen a fall in the number of job opportunities. Where jobs exist they tend to require basic education; in addition, informants felt that ethnic background and 'connections' have become paramount, virtually excluding Roma from employment (Oxfam research, July 1996).

In addition, there is evidence that paid jobs, such as domestic work, traditionally carried out by Roma women, have been taken over by other displaced women. Many of them come from rural areas and are relatively uneducated. Agencies working with displaced women have developed marketing services to assist them in securing work, neglecting to consider the impact of this on Roma women who have previously performed these jobs (communication, Dinka Masic, 1998).

The economic crisis has led to many women adopting emergency survival mechanisms, including an increased incidence of begging. Around 60 per cent of the Roma female population now beg on a regular basis (at least five times a week) (Oxfam research, July 1996). Begging is seen as a traditional way of earning income which is women's responsibility. Bosnian informants in the research, from outside the Roma communities as well as within, rationalised this division of labour as logical in that women and older people were less physically strong and unable to support themselves, while men, who are 'physically stronger and healthy, should work' (non-Roma respondent, ibid).

Informants agreed that before the war, prostitution among Roma was virtually unheard of (although prejudice in wider society led to allegations that it took place). However, informants who participated in further research (which took place in November and December 1997, with 40 women, 25 children and 20 men) revealed that, while the majority of Roma women who practise prostitution are single or heads of household, it is not uncommon for married women to resort to prostitution in order to support their families. Informants said that Roma men find this abhorrent, but at the same time expect women to provide for the family.

M.S., who is married with three small children, reported that she occasionally uses prostitution as a means to feed her family.

'My husband knows I do this and he beats me every time, but he still expects me to earn enough money to buy food and alcohol for him. I have no choice, this would never have happened before the war. Before the war, if we had no means of income, we would have simply moved on, now it is not possible, I am trapped'(personal communication 1997).

Growth in domestic violence
Domestic violence has been a feature of life in Roma communities since before the conflict; respondents attributed the causes to the economic position of Roma people, lack of education, and male alcoholism (Masic 1996), but substantial research was never done into the issue; it is therefore impossible to measure whether violence has increased post-conflict (personal communication, Dinka Masic, 1998). However, some women in our research mentioned that domestic violence has increased in the Roma community, although none would openly talk about it. The prevalent factors behind the perceived post-war increase was attributed to unemployment among Roma men, a breakdown in the structure of Roma society, and a shift in gender relations, brought about by women being the 'breadwinners'. Roma men have difficulty coming to terms with the change in relationships. In male-headed households, even while women are increasingly the main providers of income, it is still the men who have control over the economic resources. Respondents felt that, by placing the burden of economic provision on women without giving up control of the resulting resources, men are trying to maintain their power; in this light it appears that the status of women has decreased in Roma society, rather than increased.

Single women heading households
For many widowed women, movement is impossible since social norms in the Roma community will not allow women to move alone. Single-parent households rely on the close-knit Roma community to protect and

support them. In single women's households, a man from another household often controls the economic resources. Control also extends to women's social behaviour, including where they can go and who they speak to. While many women found this uncomfortable, some did express pleasure about the relative 'freedom' singledom offered them. A.C., a widow for three years with two small children, stated:'although I do not have complete control over my life, I never had that anyway. This way, I am able to move with the community and enjoy the benefits of the community without being isolated. I have never had to be a prostitute, the other women have always helped me.'

Girls' education

Social discrimination against Roma people not only takes the form of popular prejudice; informants also discussed their experiences of institutionalised discrimination, for example in education and health care. The war in Bosnia-Hercegovina has caused a crisis in basic service provision. For example, attendance at school was always relatively low for Roma children before the conflict. This was because, first, the education they received was not in their mother tongue. While some Romany-language schools opened in 1983, the quality was generally seen as poor because of the shortage of teachers trained to teach in Romany. Other schools who receive Roma children seldom offer them additional support to improve their performance and decrease the number of drop-outs.

Second, children's attendance is restricted if, as is often the case, they are expected to take on the role of providers for the family. Informants attributed low school attendance largely to the movement of the population from one area to another (Masic 1996).

Both before and after the conflict, schools hide behind a rhetoric of encouraging Roma children's education as a priority. When Oxfam, together with Radd Barnen, started a pilot project encouraging Roma

parents in one settlement in Tuzla to send their children to school, the headmaster of one school set up an obstacle, declaring that children from that settlement did not fall into the school's catchment area. After long negotiations with the school authorities, four Roma children were accepted in the school (personal communication).

This discrimination in service provision links with the strongly patriarchal culture of Roma communities and expectations of girl children to work rather than attend school, to the disadvantage of women and girls. The pre-war figure estimates the literacy rate of women was 34 per cent in comparison with a male rate of around 80 per cent. At the time of Oxfam's research, 66 per cent of boys attended school, compared to only 13 per cent of girls (all data from the Centre for Social Work, Tuzla).

Informants attributed a dramatic fall in the literacy rate to the fact that female children are now expected to beg: the literacy rate among our respondents leads us to estimate that the literacy rate of Roma women may be just 4 per cent (Oxfam research, July 1996 although not official figures). One 14-year-old girl, S.A., gets up at 5.00am every morning to go to the woods to collect fuelwood for heating and cooking; afterwards, she and her sister spend the entire day begging on the streets of Tuzla. S.A. stated: 'we have to help my mother, we can not go to school, it is our responsibility as women to provide for our brothers and father.' (Masic 1996).

Addressing the issues

Since the research was undertaken, Oxfam GB, led by the programme manager Dinka Masic, who speaks Romany, has worked with groups of Roma people on small-scale grassroots initiatives and promoted the involvement of members of the community in all other areas of Oxfam's work.

The mushrooming of local NGOs in the post-conflict period has not passed the Roma communities by; the first association of Roma people in Bosnia-Hercegovina,

62

SAE ROMA, was established in September 1996, and has been supported by Oxfam GB in line with its priority of promoting the formation of community groups. Since then, four other organisations have been formed by Roma people in the Tuzla area. This has had the negative effect of creating competition for resources, rather than creating a united voice for Roma people to advocate positive change. However, this should be understood in the context of a vast number of international aid agencies funding work in Bosnia, and promoting the growth of local organisations as an element of the process of 'democratisation'. For local people, this creation of organisations may be a very effective mechanism for survival, potentially opening up possibilities of employment in a context where this is very scarce (personal communication, Dinka Masic, 1998).

Among other activities, SAE-ROMA is carrying out a census of Roma people, and campaigning and advocating on people's basic right to essential resources including shelter, food, water, health-care and education. In particular, the association is working to challenge prejudiced attitudes to Roma people. Education for children was the starting point for practical work. The project involved basic language training for the children in Serbo-Croat, to help them to reach the standard required to enter school (in the absence of support from government, the wider agenda of the promotion of the Romany language and Roma culture has not yet been addressed). The success of this literacy project encouraged other agencies to become involved.

Addressing the interests and needs of women and gender relations in the Roma community remains a high priority for Oxfam. Oxfam uses its work with children as an 'entry point' to involve women, by encouraging them to help their children learn. Literacy classes have also been started for women; in addition to the immediate goal of literacy, the classes are intended to prepare the way for the formation of a women's group to discuss the wider issues (personal communication, Dinka Masic, 1998). In

future we hope to initiate discussions around themes such as domestic violence, prostitution, and alcoholism.

Building trust
The most valuable lesson learnt during the work thus far is the importance of allowing a long period of time to build trust and confidence between the Roma community and outsiders; projects limited by timeframes are not viable. This makes work with Roma people unattractive to many donors who are looking for quick impact.

Dialogue with Roma women remains difficult. There are no women's groups at present, and men dominate the activities of the association. It is hoped that women will become increasingly involved in the activities of the main association (as their particpation is deliberately kept low by the men involved), and perhaps, in the future, form their own group. They could then begin to address some of the issues of concern for them as women, and participation in a group would build their confidence, to enable them to address these issues in a more 'mainstream way'.

Alex Jones is Deputy Regional Representative, Eastern Europe for Oxfam GB based in Sarajevo: Kotromanica 48, 71000 Sarajevo, Bosnia-Hercegovina email: oxfam_sa@hhotmail.com

References
Crowe D, *A history of the gypsies of Eastern Europe and Russia*, 1996, St Martin's Press
Masic D, 'Report on the situation of Roma people in Tuzla Municipality', July 1996, Oxfam unpublished document

Notes

1 With thanks to Dinka Masic and Usha Kar, for reading and providing additional information
2 NDH and the other puppet regime of Serbia were established in 1941, when forces from Germany, Italy, Bulgaria, Hungary and Romania invaded Yugoslavia

Resources

compiled by Sara Chamberlain

Further reading

The Traffic in Women: Human Realities of the International Sex Trade, Siriporn Skrobanek, Nattaya Boonpakdi, and Chutima Janthakeero, 1997, Zed Books,
7 Cynthia Street, London N1 9JF, UK.
Explores the nature, extent and reaons for the global traffic in women. Based on research by the Foundation for Women in Thailand, it argues that trafficked women can only be understood via a number of different perspectives: as migrant workers, as prostitutes, and as women in a male-dominated socity.

A Matter of Honour: Experiences of Turkish Women Immigrants, by Tory Kocturk, 1993, Zed Books, 7 Cynthia Street, London N1 9JF, UK.
In Europe today there are more than 3 million Turkish workers, largely from rural areas. Nearly all of them arrived in the 1960s and 1970s. This book examines the social and cultural impact of Western industrial society on these Muslim immigrants, especially in terms of gender and family relations.

The Trade in Domestic Workers: Causes, Mechanisms and Consequences of International Migration, edited by Noeleen Hyzer, Geertje Lychlama a Nijeholt and Nedra Weerakoon, 1994, Zed Books, 7 Cynthia Street, London N1 9JF, UK.
Provides an overview and synthesis of the causes, mechanisms, and consequences of the trade in domestic workers. Analyses the interrelated structural forces, both international and national, including the role of the state, and the individual situation of women migrant workers within the family, household, and wider kinship and community networks. Traces the full cycle of migration, from sending to receiving countries.

Gender and Migration in Developing Countries, edited by Sylvia Chant,1992, Bolivian Press, 25 Floral Street, London, UK.
One of the first systematic attempts to explore the causes, nature and consequences of gender-selective population movement in a range of developing countries. Particular attention is paid to women's experiences as migrants and/ or as members of households from which men migrate. Case studies from Latin America, the Caribbean, Africa, and Asia illustrate the diversity of gender-selective migration, and also the similarities, in particular the constraints on movement of low-income women.

Migrant Women: Crossing Boundaries and Changing Identities, edited by Gina Buijs, 1993, Berg, 150 Cowley Road, Oxford, OX 1JJ, UK.
Most of the women studied in this book hoped to retain their original culture and lifestyle but found that the exigencies of being migrants and refugees forced them to examine their preconceptions and to adopt roles, both social and economic, which they would have rejected at home. This was often a traumatic experience with serious repercussions on their relationships with their menfolk. But for

some women, emigration provided a means of achieving a social and economic mobility that they would have been denied at home.

Human Capital: International Migration and Traffic in Women, Siriporn Skrobanek, 1996, SHARI, Unit 3 Canonbury Yard, New North Road, London NO 7BJ, UK.
This paper shows how the rights of migrant women in Asia are violated. It discusses the definition of trafficking in international conventions, and the legal and illegal mechanisms by which women are brought from Thailand to work in other countries, and makes recommendations for international action to prevent trafficking.

Labour Exchange: Patterns of Migration in Asia, Bridget Anderson, 1997, SHARI, Unit 3 Canonbury Yard, New North Road, London NO 7BJ, UK.
This book looks at the context in which women are now moving to find work within Asia, how they are exploited, how immigration legislation, debt and recruitment methods affect their living and working conditions, and how governments are responding.

In the Absence of Their Men : The Impact of Male Migration on Women, by Leela Gulati, 1994, SAGE Publications Ltd., 6 Bonhill Street, London, EC2A 4PU, UK.
The author focuses on the women left behind by men migrating to West Asia for work. She discusses the problems these women face, and how social change occurs in a society when men migrate. Profiles of ten women highlight various coping strategies, in differing social, economic and demographic circumstances.

Internal Migration of Women in Developing Countries, 1993, United Nations Publications, Sales and Marketing Section Room DC2-853, Dept. I004, New York, N.Y. 10017, USA.
In relation to the changing roles and status of women, this book examines why women migrate; the consequences of migration; and development and policy implications.

Women and Seasonal Labour Migration, Indo-Dutch Studies on Development Alternatives series, volume 16, edited by Loes Schenk-Sandbergen, 1995, SAGE Publications Ltd. 6 Bonhill Street, London, EC2A 4PU, UK.
Explores the gender-specific causes and consequences of seasonal rural labour migration with specific reference to the Indian states of Orissa, Kerala, Gujarat and Maharashtra. Provides an overview of the gender dimension in migration studies, and presents case studies of three types of transformation processes related to different socioeconomic, cultural and ecological systems: forest, sea and land. The strategies adopted by a women's organisation to reduce seasonal migration are outlined.

Migration of Women: The Methodological Issues in the Measurement and Analysis of Internal and International Migration, 1995, United Nations Publications, Sales and Marketing Section Room DC2-853, Dept. I004, New York, N.Y. 10017, USA.
An in-depth look at the problems that contribute to the neglect of research on women's migration. Suggests how to improve statistics and indicators on migration, eliminating many biases and misrepresentations. A new and invaluable book on a much-neglected topic.

Migration to the Arab World: Experience of Returning Migrants, 1990, United Nations Publications, Sales and Marketing Section Room DC2-853, Dept. I004, New York, N.Y. 10017, USA.
This study is a companion to 'Migration of Asian Workers to the Arab World'. The Arab region has seen a massive inflow of migrant workers from Bangladesh, India, Pakistan, Sri Lanka, Korea, the Philippines and Thailand. This book is the output from research with 500 returned migrants from these countries, to learn what problems were encountered in the pre- and post- migration periods and during their stay in the host countries.

'For the sake of the children: gender migration in the former soviet union', article by Hilary Pilkington in *Post-Soviet Women: from the Baltic to Central Asia*, edited by Mary Buckley, 1997, Cambridge University Press, The Edinburough Building, Cambridge, CB2 2RU, UK.

Investigates forced migration within the former Soviet Union after 1990, and how concern for the future of their children pushed many women to leave their homes. Examine their efforts to make a living in their new surroundings. Argues that their experiences of resettlement in Russia challenges existing Western interpretations of the gendered nature of migration which focus on displacement as leading to a loss of masculine identity, whilst having an emancipatory impact on women.

Women's Life Worlds: Women's Narratives on Shaping their Realities, edited by Edith Sizoo, Routledge, 11 New Fetter Lane, London EC4P 4EE, USA.
Presents personal narratives by 15 women of different ages and from a range of cultural, religious, social and geographical backgrounds. Challenges traditional assumptions of how women, feel about womanhood, life, society, culture and religion.

Gendered Transitions: Mexican Experiences of Immigration, Pierrette Hondagneu-Sotelo, 1994, University of California Press, 2120 Berkeley Way, Berkeley, CA 94720 U.S.A.
Includes chapters on Immigration, Gender, and settlement; The history of Mexican undocumented settlement in the United States; The Oakview barrio; Gendered transitions; Reconstructing gender through immigration and settlement; Women consolidating settlement; Gendered immigration.

International Migration in Central and Eastern Europe and the Commonwealth of Independent States, 1996, United Nations Publications, Sales and Marketing Section Room DC2-853, Dept. 1004, New York, N.Y. 10017
A powerful book which will contribute to the understanding of the new patterns of international migration, and provide a useful base for informed policy formulation and analysis. It supplies timely and objective information and explores the causes and consequences of international migration throughout the region.

International Migration: Regional Processes and Responses, 1994,United Nations Publications,

Sales and Marketing Section Room DC2-853, Dept. I004, New York, N.Y. 10017, USA.
Explains the process, causes and consequences of population movements worldwide, and identifies appropriate policy responses. It covers Africa, the Middle East, Latin America and North America and deals with migration patterns and their causes; implications for receiving and sending countries; adjustment and integration processes and policies; refugees.

Proclaiming Migrant Rights, The New International Convention on the Protection of the Rights of All Migrant Workers and Members of Their Families, Churches' Committee for Migrants in Europe and the World Council of Churches.
Available from the World Council of Churches Acct. 481 021 0001. WCC/CICARWS, Migration Secretariat, P.O. Box 2100,1211 Geneva 2, Switzerland. In English, Spanish or French.

A Moment to Choose: Risking to be with Uprooted People, Statement on Uprooted People, World Council of Churches, Refugee and Migration Service, Program Unit IV — Sharing and Service, World Council of Churches, 150 Route de Ferney, P.O. Box 2100, 1211 Geneva 2, Switzerland.
From a process of consultation and dialogue, with concerns contributed by nearly 100 national and international church bodies. In English, French, German and Spanish.

The Dynamics of 'Race and Gender: Some Feminist Interventions, edited by Haleh Afshar and Mary Maynard, 1994, Taylor and Francis Ltd., 4 John St, London, WC1N 2ET, UK.
Explores the consequences of racism for women from different backgrounds and the complexities and varieties of the forms of oppression which arise.

Worlding Women: A Feminist International Politics, Jan Jindy Pettman, 1996, Routledge, 11 New Fetter Lane, London EC4P 4EE, UK.
What can the experience of a Filipina 'mail-order bride' living in Sydney, Australia add to international polititical theory? A lot, according to the author. She develops a broad picture

of women in colonial and post-colonial relations; in racialised, ethnic and national identity conflicts; in wars and liberation movements; and in the international political economy.

Islamic Britain; Religion, Politics and Identity Among British Muslims, Philip Lewis 1994, I.B Tauris and Co Ltd, 45 Bloomsbury Square, London WC1A 2HY, UK.
How do British Muslims think about themselves, their religion and their politics? What dilemmas do they face as they give up the 'myth of return' that sustained the first generation immigrants and struggle to define a British Islam? This book challenges the sensationalist media images that have sometimes sought to portray British Muslims as a bridgehead in the West for the establishment of an Islamic theocracy.

Circle of Light: The Autobiography of Kiranjit Ahluwalia, Kiranjit Ahluwalia and Rahila Gupta, 1997, Harper Collins, 77–85 Fulham Palace Road, Hammersmith, London W6 8JB, UK.
Born into a well-off family in India, Kiranjit Ahluwalia immigrated to England in 1979 to marry a man she hardly knew. The next 10 years were a nightmare of constant physical and mental abuse at the hands of her husband. In 1989, driven beyond endurance, Kiranjit killed him. She was found guilty of murder and sentenced to life imprisonment. After a campaign coordinated by the Southall Black Sisters, she was set free in 1992.

Black British Feminism: A Reader, edited by Heidi Safia Mirza, 1997, Routledge,11 New Fetter Lane, London EC4P 4EE, UK.
The essays in this collection bring new critical insights to bear upon analyses of gendered and racialised exclusion, 'black' identity, and social and cultural difference. The specific topics discussed include 'mixed-race' identity, cultural hybridity, and postcolonial space.

The Immigration Reader, edited by David Jacobson, 1989, Blackwells Ltd, 108 Cowley Road, Oxford, OX4 1JF, UK.
Explores immigration in the US from its early history to contemporary controversies. With sections on the history of immigration in the United States, ethnicity, and comparative cross-national perspectives and political debates, the collection introduces immigration as a process which has shaped and continues to shape life in the US and American identity.

Temporary Workers or Future Citizens? Japanese and US Migration Policies, by Tadashi Hanami & Myron Weiner, 1997, Macmillan Press Limited, Brunel Road, Houndmills, Basingstoke, Hampshire, UK.
Examines the approaches of Japan and USA in dealing with employer demand for labour, control over illegal migration, the challenge of incorporating immigrants, the legal rights and social benefits of foreign residents and illegal migrants, and the claims of refugees and asylum seekers.

The Politics of Immigration and Race, Andrew Geddes, 1996, Baseline Book Company, P.O. Box 34, Chorlton, Manchester, M21 9LL, UK.
In recent British history, immigration and associated issues of 'race' and racism have been at the heart of political debate, generating controversy among people from different backgrounds and perspectives. The book gives a detailed analysis of the history of immigration into Britain, immigration and race relation policy, party politics, political participation and 'race', developments in other European countries, and the Europeanisation of British immigration policy.

Southern China: Migrant Workers and Economic Transformation, Angie Knox, 1997, CIIR, Unit 3, Canonbury Yard, 190a New North Road, London N1 7BJ, UK.
Gives an overview of the shift in China from a planned to a market economy which has propelled it to its position as the world's fastest-growing economy. It focuses on the southern coast, analysing the region's contribution to China's remarkable economic growth. It questions the resulting social costs, and the government's apparent view that migrant labour is a resource to be exploited in the interests of attracting foreign investment and developing the economy.

British Immigration Policy since 1939:
The Making of Multi-Racial Britain, Ian
R.G.Spencer, 1997, Routledge, 11 New
Fetter Lane, London EC4P 4EE, UK.
In less than 50 years, Britain has shifted from
being a virtually all-white society to one in which
ethnicity and race are significant social and
political factors. The book traces this transition.
Spencer documents the restrictive measures
which failed to prevent the rapid influx in the
late 1950s and 1960s of people of various nation-
alities, who displayed considerable initiative in
overcoming obstacles placed in their way.

Imposing Aid: Emergency Assistance for Refugees,
Barbara Harrell-Bond, 1986, although out of
print, is available on floppy disk from the
Refugee Studies Programme, Oxford University
(see organisations for contact details).
This publication looks at refugee migrants
and the impact of food delays on Ugandan
refugees in Sudan, which forced them back to
abandoned fields or to forage for food, caused
massive malnutrition and hindered their
progress towards self-reliance.

Journals and Newsletters

Network News: Fall 1997, issue on Gender and
Migration. Includes articles on Structural
Adjustment Undermines Social Welfare
Around the World: Women in the Global
Labor Market, By Grace Chang; Transnational
Motherhood, By Pierette Hondagneu-Sotelo;
Domestic Workers ORGANIZE!, by Cristina
Riegos; Women's Health, Immigration, and
Population, by Betsy Hartmann.

Migration News: summarises the most important
immigration and integration developments of
the preceding month. Topics are grouped by
region. Many issues also contain summaries
and reviews of recent research publications. A
paper edition is available by mail for $30
domestic and $50 foreign for one year and $55
and $95 for a two-year subscription. Make
cheques payable to UC Regents and send to:
Philip Martin, Department of Agricultural
Economics, University of California, Davis,

California 95616, USA. If you wish to subscribe
by e-mail, send your email address to:
migrant@primal.ucdavis.edu. There is no
charge for email subscriptions. Current and
back issues may be accessed via Internet on
the Migration News Web page at:
http://migration.ucdavis.edu.

Asian Migrant Forum: articles on migration
throughout Asia, from Asian Migrant Centre.
To subscribe to Asian Migrant Forum, Asian
Immigrant Bulletin and other AMC occasional
publications, write to the Asian Migrant
Centre, Ltd., No. 4 Jordan Road, Kowloon,
Hong Kong. Or e-mail amc@hk.super.net for
more information. ubscription rates within
Asia are US$ 30, Outside Asia — US$ 50.

AIWA Newsletter: a newsletter of Asian
Immigrant Women Advocates (see organisa-
tions). To receive the AIWA newsletter, write:
AIWA, 310 Eighth Street, Ste. 301, Oakland,
CA 94607, or e-mail: aiwa@igc.apc.org.

IOM Latin America Migration Journal: A
bilingual publication on migration produced
by the Center for Information on Migration in
Latin America (CIMAL — for contact information see organisations). Is distributed to 1500
world subscribers, and is available at the
CIMAL Web site: http://www.renua.cl/oim

*The Journal of Immigration and Nationality Law
and Practice.* The Journal, edited by ILPA (see
organisations for contact details) appears
quarterly and includes in-depth articles on
aspects of immigration, asylum and nationality
law and practice worldwide and summaries
of important cases.

Know Your Rights: brochures in English and
Spanish on domestic workers' rights, pregnancy
discrimination, sex discrimination, and race
and gender discrimination. Contact Equal
Rights Advocates, 1663 Mission St.,Suite 550,
San Francisco, CA 94103, telephone 010 415
621-0672. Free for up to 10 brochures; over 10
brochures will cost the price of postage.

Videos

A Life Without Fear: a video about a South Asian woman experiencing domestic violence in America and the ways in which she deals with her situation. From SAKHI, P.O. Box 20208, Greeley Square Station, New York, NY 10001, USA, telephone 010 212 695-5447.

Mujer Valorate: (Woman, Believe in Yourself), documentary video about domestic violence, the law and remedies available for battered Latina women in Washington DC. To order, make cheque or money order payable to: Hermanas Unidas, Ayuda Inc., 1736 Columbia Rd. N.W., Washington D.C. 20009, USA. Price: $20.00, shipping $4.00. Telephone 010 202 387-4848.

New World Border: documents the increasing militarisation of the US/Mexico border and the consequences for human rights. Includes interviews with border activists and testimony from immigrants, and provides an analysis of free trade policies and their impacts on migration, and current efforts to build solidarity. Copies cost $20.00 for individuals and $50.00 for institutions plus $3.00 shipping and handling. To order write to: The National Network for Immigrant and Refugee Rights, 310 8th Street, Suite 307, Oakland, CA 94607, USA.

Sisters and Daughters Betrayed: A video about the realities of sex trafficking and forced prostitution. It examines the economics of trafficking and the parallels between the situation in Asia and in other world regions. It presents interviews with activist women in Asia who are involved in campaigns against trafficking. Send cheques for US $8 to: The Global Fund for Women, 425 Sherman Avenue, Suite 300, Palo Alto, CA 94306, USA.

Organisations

The International Organization for Migration
IOM is committed to the principle that humane and orderly migration benefits migrants and society. IOM acts with its partners in the international community to assist in meeting the operational challenges of migration; advance understanding of migration issues; encourage social and economic development through migration; and uphold the human dignity and well-being of migrants. The programmes is divided into four main areas: humanitarian migration, migration for development, technical co-operation, and migration debate, research and information.

Anti-Slavery International (ASI)
The Stableyard, Broomgrove Road, London SW9 9TL, Britain Tel: (44) 171 924 9555; fax: (44) 171 738 4110.
Web site: http://www.charitynet.org/~asi/
ASI promotes the eradication of slavery and slavery-like practices. The abuses which ASI opposes include: slavery and the buying and selling of people as objects; trafficking of women and the predicament of migrant workers who are trapped into servitude; debt bondage and other traditions which force people into low status work; forced labour; forced prostitution; abusive forms of child labour; and early or forced marriage and other forms of servile marriage. ASI focuses on the rights of people who are particularly vulnerable to exploitation of their labour, notably women, children, migrant workers and indigenous peoples. ASI collects information about these abuses, brings them to the attention of the public and promotes public action to end them; identifies ways in which these abuses can be brought to an end, and influences policy-makers in governments or other institutions at national and international level to take action accordingly; supports victims of the abuses which ASI opposes in their struggle for freedom, in particular by working with organisations they establish and other organisations campaigning on their behalf.

The Global Alliance Against the Traffic in Women (GAATW)
The International Coordination Office, P.O.Box 1281, Bangkok Post Office, Bangkok 10500, Thailand.
Tel. (662) 864-1427-8, fax. (662) 864-1637.
Email: gaatw@mozart.inet.co.th
Web Site: http://www.inet.co.th/org/gaatw
GAATW was formed at the International Work-

shop on Migration and Traffic in Women organised by the Foundation for Women in Chiangmai, Thailand, in October 1994. GAATW's aim is not to stop the migration of women but to ensure that human rights of women are taken into consideration by authorities and agencies involved. Promotes the involvement of grassroots women in all work against this form of modern slavery so that any work done addresses the real problem and does not aggravate their vulnerable situation.

Kalayaan (justice for overseas domestic workers) St Francis Community Centre, Pottery Lane, London W11 4NQ, UK. Tel: (44) (0)171 243 2942, fax: (0)171 792 3060 E-mail: 100711.2262@compuserve.com Since 1987, Kalayaan has been working for the restoration of fundamental workers rights to overseas domestic workers in the UK and Europe. Kalayaan's work to change policy and support domestic workers has included the systematic documentation of over 2000 case studies; the provision of services, support and legal referral for escaped workers; lobbying the British government, European Parliament and UN to address contemporary forms of slavery; working with the media; and mobilising support for domestic works from individuals and organisations, including community groups, trade unions such as the ICFTU, and trade union bodies such as the ILO.

Asian Immigrant Women Advocates (AIWA) 310 Eighth Street #301, Oakland, CA 94607, USA. Tel: (510) 268-0192, fax: (510) 268-0194. Email: aiwa@igc.apc.org Asian Immigrant Women Advocates (AIWA) is a community based organisation established in 1983. Through education, leadership development, and organising, AIWA seeks to foster the empowerment of low-income, limited-English speaking Asian immigrant women who work in the greater San Francisco, Oakland, and South Bay Area. Seeks to help women to develop the skills to advocate for justice and dignity in their lives and workplaces.

The Mission for Filipino Migrant Workers (MFMW) http://www.hk.super.net/~migrant/index.htm

St. John's Cathedral, Garden Road, Central, Hong Kong.Telephone : (852) 2552-8264, fax : (852) 2526-2894 E-mail : migrant@hk.super.net An ecumenical institution established to work with Filipino migrant workers in Hong Kong in their struggle for better working and living conditions. Founded in 1981, it extends support services to both individuals and various migrant organisations.

Aji-kon (The Forum on Asian Migrant Workers) c/o NCC 2-3-18-24 Nishiwaseda Shinjuku-ku, Tokyo 169 JAPAN. Tel 00 81-3-3207-7801, fax 00 81-3-3204-9495. E-mail:ajikon@jca.or.jp Founded in 1987, Aji-Kon works to solve the problems of migrant labourers in Japan. It has published a handbook for migrant workers in English, Korean and Persian with PARC (Pacific Asia Resource Center), as well as other books about migrant workers in Japan. Aji-Kon has held nationwide meetings about negative changes in Japanese labour and migration laws, and about violence by Immigration Bureau officers. Aji-Kon publishes a monthly newsletter *Migrant Workers' News*

The National Network for Immigrant and Refugee Rights (NNIRR, 310 8th Street, Suite 307, Oakland, CA 94607, USA. Tel: 010 510 465-1984, fax: 010 510 465-1885. E-mail: nnirr@nnirr.org Web URL: http://www.nnirr.org NNIRR is composed of local coalitions and immigrant, community, religious, civil rights and labour organisations and activists. It serves as a forum to share information and analysis, to educate communities and the general public, and to develop and coordinate plans of action on important immigrant and refugee issues. The organisation works to promote a just immigration and refugee policy in the U.S. and to defend and expand the rights of all immigrants and refugees, regardless of immigration status.

Center for information on migration in Latin America (CIMAL) Casilla 781, Santiago, Chile. Tel 00 562 274 67 13.

Fax 00 562 204 97 04. E-mail: CIMAL@REUNA.CL
Website: http://www.reuna.cl/oim
CIMAL is a specialised information resource
on international migration in Latin America,
the Caribbean and other geographical areas.
CIMAL collects, reviews and write abstracts
for documents written about international
migration. Its resources include 10,000 documents
with the latest information on international
migration (policy, legislation, administration,
refugees, illegal immigration, border migration,
women migrants and humanitarian assistance);
the main specialised journals, world press
clippings on the subject; a bibliographic data
base with document abstracts, a data base
with the names of migration experts and
institutions, and various CD-ROMS.

*Ecumenical Documentation and Information
Centre for Eastern and Southern Africa* (EDICESA)
P.O. Box H. 94, Hartfield, Harare, Zimbabwe.
Tel: 00 263 457 0311/2, fax 00 263 457 979.
E-mail: edicesa@mango.zw
Has an extensive library and large documen-
tation department which collects information
on refugee and migration related issues in
Eastern and Southern Africa. EDICESA works
with Churches and international organisations
to support the advocacy and activism that is
necessary to bring about change in this region.

Immigration Law Practitioners' Association (ILPA)
Lindsey House , 40/42 Charterhouse Street,
London EC1M 6JH. Tel: 00 44 171 251 8383,
fax: 00 44 171 251 8384.
Email: ilpa@mcr1.poptel.org.uk.
http://www.ein.org.uk/ilpa/
ILPA is the UK's professional association of
lawyers and academics practising in or concerned about immigration, asylum and nationality
law. ILPA aims to promote and improve the
advising and representation of immigrants; to
provide information to members on the law
and practice relating to immigration and
nationality; to secure a non-racist, non-sexist,
just and equitable system of immigration and
national law. ILPA organises training courses
throughout the UK on various aspects of
immigration and nationality law. ILPA
presents views of immigration lawyers on law

and practice in the field to MPs and
government departments. In association with
similar professional associations in other EC
member states, ILPA is developing a network
of immigration lawyers throughout Europe to
promote the exchange of information on
national law and practice in this field and
developments at the European level.

Immigration Advisory Service
Head Office, 3rd Floor, County House, 190
Great Dover Street, London SE1 4YB
Tel: 00 44 171 357 7511, fax: 0171 403 5875.
IAS is the largest, most experienced charity
giving free advice and representation in
immigration and asylum matters in Britain.
Regional offices are in Birmingham, Cardiff,
Central London, Gatwick, Glasgow, Hounslow,
Leeds and Manchester. An IAS duty
counsellor is available 24 hours a day on
(44)(0)171 378 9191.

International Labour Organisation (ILO)
Migration Branch (MIGRANT)
Tel: 00 41 22 799 6413, fax: 00 41 22 799 7657.
E-mail: bohning@ilo.or
http://www.ilo.org/public/english/60empf
or/migrant/cont1.htm
Objectives of the ILO's Migration Branch are
to provide ILO constituents with enhanced
capacities to adopt policies and measures which
improve the conditions under which desired
migration takes place; and ameliorate the
integration of migrants and their families.
Main activities are to help governments to form-
ulate and evaluate policies, to draft legislation
or develop procedures, to collect data on the
admission and rights of foreign workers; to
counter discrimination in enterprises; to help
trade unions through workers' education
seminars and by organising visits to other
unions to learn from them or to collaborate
with them. Cooperation with universities,
research bodies and NGOs is also sought.

Human Rights Watch
350 Fifth Avenue, 34th Floor New York, NY,
10118-3299 USA, Tel: 00 212 290-4700,
fax: 00 212 736-1300. E-mail: hrwnyc@hrw.org
http://www.hrw.org/

Human Rights Watch is dedicated to protecting the human rights of people around the world, to prevent discrimination, to uphold political freedom, to protect people from inhumane conduct in wartime, and to bring offenders to justice. It investigates and exposes human rights violations. It challenges governments and those who hold power to end abusive practices and respect international human rights law. It enlists the public and the international community to support the cause of human rights for all.

Stonewall Immigration Group
16 Clerkenwell Close, London EC1R 0AA, UK. Telephone 0171 336 8880, fax 0171 336 8864. E-mail: info@stonewall.org.uk
http://www.stonewall.org.uk/contents.html/
The aim of the Stonewall Immigration Group is to work for a change in the immigration rules and practice to ensure that same-sex couples have the same immigration rights as heterosexual couples.

The Commission for Filipino Migrant Workers
St Francis Centre, Pottery Lane,
London W11 4NQ.
Telephone: 0171 221 0356, Fax: 0171 792 3060
CFMW funds a variety of courses, workshops and one-off training sessions to empower Filipino migrant workers. Course subjects include public speaking, chairing meetings, minute-taking, book-keeping, effective communications, and leadership skills. CFMW also organises health care sessions on contraception, HIV and AIDS, drugs, stress management and alternative medicine. The organisation is also running a two-year project that is training women to become advocates of women's issues to promote gender awareness and understanding throughout the Filipino community in Britain.

Forced Migration

The Refugee Council
3 Bondway, London SW8 1SJ. Tel. 00 44 171 820 3000, fax 00 44 171 582 9929.
E-mail refcounciluk@gn.apc.org

Gives practical help and promotes the rights of asylum seekers and refugees, in the UK and abroad. It advises asylum seekers and refugees about their rights; helps refugees to settle in the UK; informs advisers working with asylum seekers and refugees; supports refugee community organisations; promotes national settlement policies for asylum seekers and refugees; protects unaccompanied refugee children; trains asylum seekers and refugees for future employment; provides shelter for homeless asylum seekers; advocates on behalf of refugees and asylum seekers; makes the link between communities of asylum-seekers in the UK and conditions in their county of origin.

European Council on Refugees and Exiles (ECRE)
ECRE EU office, 72 Rue du Commerce, 1040 Brussels, Belgium. Telephone: 00 32 2 514 5939 fax: 00 32 2 514 5922. E-mail: EUECRE@ecre.be
ECRE is an organisation established in 1973 for co-operation between more than 50 non-governmental organisations in Europe concerned with refugees. ECRE's objective is to promote, through joint analysis, research and information exchange, a humane and generous asylum policy in Europe. ECRE's principal activities are policy analysis and advocacy, legal analysis and networking, information and documentation, Central and Eastern European programme, and biannual general meetings.

Refugee Studies Programme
Queen Elizabeth House, University of Oxford, 21 St Giles, Oxford OX1 3LA, UK. Tel: 00 44 1865 270723; fax: 00 44 1865 270721. E-mail: RSP@QEH.OX.AC.UK Web site:
http://www.qeh.ox.ac.uk/rsp/
Part of the University of Oxford's International Development Centre. Its aim is to increase understanding of the causes and consequences of forced migration through research, teaching, publications, seminars and conferences, and to provide a forum for discussion between researchers, practitioners and policy-makers.

International Refugee Documentation Network (IRDN) Web site:
http://userpage.fu-berlin.de/^migration/

Unites NGOS and intergovernmental institutions active in the field of refugee relief. The tasks of the IRDN are cooperation in monitoring refugee and migrant flows, early identification of problem situations, and the exchange of information and data concerning refugees and asylum. The IRDN also warns decision-makers about the problems of refugee relief and refugee movements. At the moment the IRDN is hosted by the Berlin Institute for Social Research (BIVS). For further information: emz@compuserve.com

The Danish Refugee Council (DRC)
Borgergade 10, 3rd floor, P.O. Box 53,
DK-1002, Copenhagen K, Denmark.
Tel: 00 45 33 912700, fax: 00 45 33 328448.
E-mail: drc@nordnet.se.
A private humanitarian association consisting of 21 cooperative organisations, including the Danish Red Cross and Save the Children. Was established in 1956 to help political refugees in Denmark and internationally. DRC aims to protect refugees from persecution and to promote lasting solutions to the problems of refugees and internally displaced persons. The main tasks of the DRC are to undertake documentation, education and information activities, to advise asylum seekers and promote humanitarian development of rules of law and legal usage, to assist refugees, voluntary organisations and public authorities with the integration and possible repatriation of refugees, to raise funds for assistance in refugee situations, and to organise cooperation about and manage international relief work for refugees and exiles.

Refugee Legal Centre
Sussex House, 39/45 Bermondsey Street, London SE1 3XF, UK
An independent organisation which provides free legal advice and respresentation for asylum seekers and refugees. On a commercial basis, provides legal and other relevant information to the legal representatives of asylum seekers and refugees.

Web sites

The International Organization for Migration (IOM) Web site
http://www.iom.ch/
An electronic information clearing house of documents, data, experts, institutions, conferences, studies, legislation and other migration/related information. Comments welcome: info@iom.int

The National Network for Immigrant and Refugee Rights (NNIRR) Web site
http://www.nnirr.org
Information on the National Network, its activities and membership; online issues of Network News, the quarterly newsletter of NNIRR; News and updates on the militarisation of the US/Mexico border; concise information on immigration and immigrant and refugee issues; analysis of current legislation affecting immigrant and refugee communities; and information about the NNIRR's latest campaigns, and how you can get involved.

Migrant Rights
http://www.iom.ch/migrant_rights/
Developed by the International Organisation for Migration (IOM), and launched on the fiftieth Anniversary of the Universal Declaration on Human Rights, this Web page on Migrants' Rights is intended to share information on the rights of migrants and provide links to other useful sources.

Global Alliance Against the Trafficking of Women Web Site
http://www.inet.co.th/org/gaatw/
Includes information about GAATW, its objectives and activities; and about the Asia Pacific Plan of Action to Combat Traffic in Women, Forced Labour and Slavery-like Practices.